The AI Whisperer

Handbook for Leveraging
Conversational Artificial
Intelligence and ChatGPT for
Business

Severin Sorensen
With contributions by Amelia Chatterley

V1.3

Printed in the United States of America

First Printing, 2023

ISBN 9798391382416

www.epraxis.com

TABLE OF CONTENTS

What is an AI Whisperer?

Artificial intelligence has inspired science fiction authors for decades. The idea of the AI overlord taking control of humanity has been fodder for hundreds of pulp novels, movies, and comic books. That being the case, it's no surprise that the advent of true AI tools has been met with skepticism in most cases, and even fear in others.

This began in earnest on November 30, 2022 with OpenAI's introduction of ChatGPT.

For those who don't know, ChatGPT is a natural language processing tool driven by artificial intelligence technology that allows you to create written content, website code, emails, essays, etc. Use cases include help with decision-making, data analysis, process automation, customer support, content creation, trend prediction, team collaboration, market research, training assistance, and more.

Today, individuals communicate and direct ChatGPT and other generative conversational AI through prompts or requests that inform AI what you want it to do. For example, a user could request AI to analyze, assess, make recommendations, perform routine tasks, write articles, create ad copy, make forecasts, summarize research, create minutes and note summaries for a meeting, create training materials, receive help with using MS Excel workbook creation, and even write code in Python or Java. AI can do all that and more.

It's an extremely powerful tool that has become the topic of heated debate and has even been banned in some countries.

But is ChatGPT, and other AI platforms rapidly hitting the market, a reason to fear, or rejoice?

I posit that, much like the advent of the electric lightbulb that made candlelight a thing of the past, ChatGPT, Google Bard, and AI in general has a much greater chance to improve our businesses than it does to harm them. Given the right prompts it creates a form of superpower for the skilled user.

If you know how to use these tools, that is.

And that is where this handbook comes in.

The terms "AI whisperer" or "ChatGPT whisperer" are informal, colloquial expressions used to describe people who have an exceptional ability to interact with and understand ChatGPT, and other generative conversational AI language models.

The person who possesses such ability, can tap into the advanced knowledge of the model's inner workings, strengths, and weaknesses, effectively communicating with artificial intelligence to obtain relevant and accurate information or insights. The terms are derived from the concept of a "horse whisperer" or "dog whisperer," people known to have a unique talent for communicating with and understanding animals.

I was intrigued recently by an article appearing on Bloomberg.com written by Conrad Quilty-Harper on March 29, 2023. Under the article masthead *'$335,000 Pay for 'AI Whisperer' Jobs Appears in Red-Hot Market: The fast-growing apps have created a seller's market for anyone — even liberal arts grads — capable of manipulating its output.'*[1] Writes Quilty-Harper, *"As the technology proliferates, many companies are finding they need*

---

[1] https://www.bloomberg.com/news/articles/2023-03-29/ai-chatgpt-related-prompt-engineer-jobs-pay-up-to-335-000

someone to add rigor to their results. 'It's like an AI whisperer,'
says Albert Phelps, a prompt engineer at Mudano, part of
consultancy firm Accenture in Leytonstone, England."

In the article the author explores that a growing jobs market is emerging around large language models (LLMs), with prompt engineers sought after to coax artificial intelligence (AI) to produce better results and train workforces to harness tools. Prompt engineering emerged in 2017 when AI researchers created pre-trained LLMs, which could be adapted to a wide range of tasks with the addition of human text input. Anthropic, a Google-backed startup, and automated document reviewer Klarity, among others, are advertising for prompt engineer roles in California, with salaries up to $335,000. The best-paying roles often go to people with PhDs in machine learning or ethics, or those who have founded AI companies.

There is indeed an emerging field of 'AI Whisperers' providing richer and deeper prompt engineering for large language models, and highlights that demand for prompt engineers is growing rapidly. Companies such as Google, TikTok, and Netflix are driving up salaries in response. The article also mentioned that individuals with a background in history, philosophy, or English language are well-suited to this role, as they possess strong wordplay skills.

In short, not unlike a skilled carpenter or musician, if someone understands how to use a tool, they will produce better results faster. Creative people who know how to ask the AI programs good questions, will coax better responses and produce high-quality content more quickly. Anyone can swing a hammer and tap on a few nails or pick up a violin and make it produce a sound. However, in the right hands, a skilled carpenter can build a palace, and a master violinist can create a musical masterpiece even from an old violin.

My name is Severin Sorensen, and for most of my life, I've been an entrepreneur. Over the past 13 years, I've dedicated myself

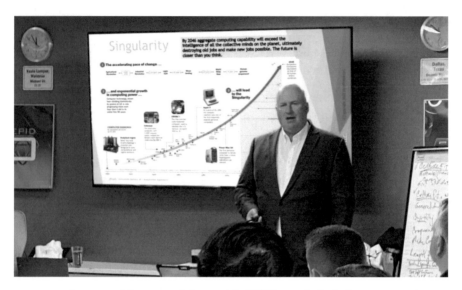

to executive coaching, working with CEOs and their key executive teams across numerous industries. Over the years, I've coached business executives at large multinational corporations like Rio Tinto, managing over $22 billion in annual revenue, to rapidly growing INC 5000 companies, along with small to medium-sized businesses with annual revenues ranging from $20 million to $750 million. These experiences along with my work with thousands of Vistage CEOs, Key Executives, Emerging Leaders, and Advancing Leaders groups, I've accumulated over 8,000 hours of paid executive coaching experience, working one-to-one with CEOs, small peer executive groups, and delivering keynote speeches and workshops on multiple continents. I've even created a website called AreteCoach.io to help executive coaches be better coaches seeking to amplify the evidence-based coaching research and practices.

Now, I don't have time to personally share with you individually what I wish to share with readers more broadly in this book. And I want to deliver the message of this book at a substantially reduced cost to you. For if you were to find time on my calendar for an executive coaching session, I'd need to charge you substantially for my time as it is scarce, limited, and precious to me.

I want to share the important information in this book as affordably as I can to reach the widest audience possible. I think it's what's needed most at this time. The information herein will help individuals, entrepreneurs, CEOs, executives, and their employees 'take the waiting out of wanting' to implement AI. And as my late coaching colleague Richard Bosworth of London, used to say, *"Information trends to be free, while implementation is what you pay for."* Let's get you the information now.

I hope the information and insights in this book will rock your world, light your creative fire, and release the hounds of curiosity in some great work. And in your use of AI, I encourage you to be good, not evil. Be mindful to be ethical in your use of AI. Fire can forge metal into shapes of great value and strength, and fire can also burn down forests if not handled carefully. Make a present intention to be good and do good. May your own AI experience be a blessing to mankind, to increase human potential, and not a curse as some AI fiction writers want us to believe.

In this spirit of abundance, I aim to share my insights on AI Whispering for small and medium-sized businesses and their employees. This book will teach you how to leverage AI assistants like ChatGPT and Google Bard to enhance ideation, questioning, critical thinking, processing, application, and implementation skills for your business.

Since 2020, my coaching and public speaking engagements have focused on introducing AI and automation topics to help businesses tackle labor shortages, empower employees, and prepare for the emerging age of AI and automation. I have closely followed the groundbreaking work on AI and robotics conducted by McKinsey and Company[2], as well as the invaluable annual reports

---

[2]   https://www.mckinsey.com/capabilities/quantumblack/our-insights/the-state-of-ai-in-2022-and-a-half-decade-in-review

from the Stanford AI Index Project[3]. It amazes me how many business leaders remain uninformed or unaware of AI's impact on their world today, despite AI advancements like ChatGPT by OpenAI being in plain sight.

During my business-focused workshops, I often witness participants' awe-struck reactions when they realize the potential of AI for their businesses. However, some still deny that AI will have any impact on their operations. With this book, I aim to ignite your imagination and insights.

I hope this serves as a catalyst for you and your employees to explore the transformative potential of AI. As an executive coach, my mission is to awaken, challenge, and inspire my clients to achieve more and attain better results. It is in this spirit that I share the essential material contained within this book.

In my opinion, AI will not entirely replace jobs; instead, it has the potential to create numerous new opportunities, including roles for fact-checkers and those skilled at utilizing AI effectively. More crucially, I believe that your job won't be replaced by AI, but rather, someone proficient in AI may take your position. To prevent this from happening, be proactive and take control of your own destiny starting today.

Be the one who acts, rather than the one acted upon.

As Professor Shelley Palmer of Advanced Media at Syracuse

---

[3] Reports have occurred in most years from 2017 to 2023. The Citation for the 2023 report is: Nestor Maslej, Loredana Fattorini, Erik Brynjolfsson, John Etchemendy, Katrina Ligett, Terah Lyons,

James Manyika, Helen Ngo, Juan Carlos Niebles, Vanessa Parli, Yoav Shoham, Russell Wald, Jack Clark,

and Raymond Perrault, "The AI Index 2023 Annual Report," AI Index Steering Committee,

Institute for Human-Centered AI, Stanford University, Stanford, CA, April 2023.

University pointed out recently, AI will be used in many industries, but not necessarily replace human workers entirely. Palmer gave an interview on CNN, stating, *"Jobs like middle managers, salespeople, writers and journalists, accountants and bookkeepers, and doctors who specialize in things like drug interactions are 'doomed' when it comes to the possibility of AI being incorporated into their jobs."* She continued by pointing out jobs like these will all use AI but not necessarily be substituted entirely. *"It's not going to replace you. Someone who knows how to use it well is going to take your job, and that's a guarantee."*[4]

The AI Whisperer was written to help you leverage the power of AI and stand out in your respective industries. By using AI tools to their advantage, you can not only keep your jobs, but do them much better, and create a new super-power in your ability to add value to your skillsets and your contribution to your businesses. This book is not just a technical manual; it is an invitation to a journey of discovery, creativity, and growth. It will teach you to harness the power of AI to solve problems, create opportunities, and elevate your business to new heights.

By learning to use sentence stems like "help me ideate," "create," "explore," "explain," "discover," "uncover," and "learn more," you will empower your AI companion to generate meaningful and insightful responses.

There's no reason to be left behind. AI is here to stay. Learn to use it and give yourself and your team the advantage they need going into the future.

Now, let's begin.

---

[4]   https://www.nbc15.com/2023/02/02/experts-say-artificial-intelligence-will-take-jobs-also-create-new-ones/

The Art of Questioning

Unlocking the Secrets of AI Communication

"The only true wisdom is in knowing you know nothing."

- Socrates

As we venture into the world of artificial intelligence, it is essential to recognize the power of asking great questions. As 'The AI Whisperer,' your ability to communicate effectively with AI systems like ChatGPT depends on your ability to craft thought-provoking, insightful questions that delve deeper into the subject matter. In this chapter, we will explore why asking great questions is crucial to better understand AI and how to use Bloom's Taxonomy, the framework for categorizing educational goals, to generate meaningful prompts.

"All men by nature desire to know."

- Aristotle

Curiosity is an innate human trait, and our relentless pursuit of knowledge has shaped our world. The same applies when interacting with AI. To unlock the true potential of these intelligent systems, we must approach them with an open mind and a thirst for knowledge. Asking great questions is essential to "whisper well" because it encourages critical thinking, promotes deeper understanding, and fosters meaningful conversations.

> *"One must learn by doing the thing; for though you think you know it, you have no certainty, until you try."*
>
> - Aristotle

Bloom's Taxonomy offers a framework for crafting questions that challenge our thinking and facilitate deeper learning. It was developed in 1956 by Benjamin Bloom, with collaborators Max Englehart, Edward Furst, Walter Hill, and David Krathwohl. This framework has been applied by generations of K-12 teachers, university instructors, and professors in their lessons.

The structure consists of six major categories: Knowledge, Comprehension, Application, Analysis, Synthesis, and Evaluation. Consider the following sentence as a starting point for engaging with AI using Bloom's Taxonomy:

- **Remembering:** "What are the key principles of...?"
- **Understanding:** "Can you explain the concept of...?"

- **Applying:** "How would you apply...in a real-world scenario?"
- **Analyzing:** "What are the underlying factors that contribute to...?"
- **Evaluating:** "What are the advantages and disadvantages of...?"
- **Creating:** "How might we innovate in the field of...to address future challenges?"

"The beginning of wisdom is the definition of terms."

\- Socrates

As you engage with AI, remember the importance of asking questions that provoke thought, encourage reflection, and inspire creativity. Keep in mind the wisdom of great thinkers:

"We can easily forgive a child who is afraid of the dark; the real tragedy of life is when men are afraid of the light."

\- Plato

As AI Whisperers, we must not be afraid to venture into the unknown, to explore new ideas, and to challenge existing beliefs. Allow yourself to be guided by the wisdom of the past:

> *"Judge a man by his questions rather than his answers."*
> - Voltaire

In integrating our insights from history, we can craft a new perspective:

> *"The greatest AI Whisperers are those who dare to ask the questions that illuminate the darkness, unveiling the true potential of intelligent machines."*
> - Severin Sorensen

As we continue, embrace an open mind and a curious heart. Imagine *'what if'* and envision the next most important step in your journey as an AI Whisperer. Let the power of questioning be your guide as you explore the infinite possibilities that await you in the world of artificial intelligence.

> *"Now, let us turn the page and discover together what new insights and breakthroughs await us as we continue our journey into the heart of AI."*
>
> – Severin Sorensen

Bloom's Taxonomy offers a framework for crafting questions that challenge our thinking and facilitate deeper learning.

Asking a good question involves a combination of several factors: clarity, relevance, depth, and purpose. A good question should be clear and concise, focusing on a specific issue or topic. It should be relevant to the subject matter at hand and contribute to the understanding or resolution of the problem. It should also encourage critical thinking and reflection, promoting deeper analysis and understanding. Lastly, a good question should have a purpose, whether it is to explore new ideas, challenge existing beliefs, or solve a problem.

Bloom's Taxonomy is a useful tool for developing better questioning expertise. It is a hierarchical classification of cognitive abilities, ranging from lower-order thinking aids to higher-order thinking skills. The six levels of Bloom's Taxonomy are:

Image courtesy of Bloom's Taxonomy[5]

- **Remembering**: Recalling facts and basic concepts.
  Questions at this level test memory and basic
  understanding.
    - o Example: "What are the main components of a
      computer?"

- **Understanding**: Explaining ideas and concepts.
  Questions at this level test comprehension and
  interpretation.

---

[5] https://bloomstaxonomy.net/

- o Example: "Can you explain the differences between a desktop computer and a laptop?"

- **Applying**: Using information in new situations. Questions at this level test the ability to apply knowledge and skills to solve problems.
  - o Example: "How would you choose the best computer for graphic design tasks?"

- **Analyzing**: Breaking information into parts to explore relationships and connections. Questions at this level test the ability to break down complex concepts and analyze their components.
  - o Example: "What factors contribute to the performance of a computer?"

- **Evaluating**: Justifying a decision or course of action. Questions at this level test the ability to make informed choices and judgments based on evidence and reasoning.
  - o Example: "What are the advantages and disadvantages of using a tablet instead of a laptop for work?"

- **Creating**: Generating new ideas, products, or ways of viewing things. Questions at this level test the ability to synthesize information and create new knowledge.
  - o Example: "How might the future of computing technology impact the way we work and communicate?"

By incorporating Bloom's Taxonomy into your questioning, you can create a more structured approach to asking questions. From there you can promote deeper understanding and critical thinking. Start by asking lower-order questions to establish a foundation of knowledge, and gradually progress to higher-order questions that challenge assumptions, encourage reflection, and inspire creativity. This approach will help you ask better questions and contribute to more meaningful discussions and problem-solving.

As you engage with AI, remember the importance of asking questions that provoke thought, encourage reflection, and inspire creativity.

As AI Whisperers, we must not be afraid to venture into the unknown, to explore new ideas, and to challenge existing beliefs. The greatest AI Whisperers will be those who dare to ask the questions that illuminate the darkness, unveiling the true potential of intelligent machines.

50 Ways Businesses Can Use ChatGPT Today

With 50 practical use cases, you'll have a wealth of opportunities to apply AI in various aspects of your business. But more than that, you will be able to approach each idea with curiosity and wonderment, opening the door to endless possibilities.

However, we must caution you: while *The AI Whisperer* aims to share the incredible potential of AI, it is essential that you review the content produced by AI personally to inspect for errors, tone, and accuracy from your own AI queries. Sometimes AI in its creative musings creates wildly inaccurate material and makes stuff up. You must be on guard for this, and fact checking is essential with AI. We have included a chapter near the close of this book titled, 'Dealing with AI Errors" that speaks more to this topic.

Additionally, we encourage you to seek advice from your own personal and business advisors before implementing any of the use cases, solutions or suggestions recommended in this book. For example, one could ask AI to offer legal or tax advice, and it will often give what appears to be valuable information; however, we strongly recommend that you have your own attorney, legal, and tax advisors review any AI recommendations before using them directly.

Furthermore, in this book we share our AI Whisperer wisdom with an attitude of abundance. As the author, there are likely errors in this book, either from our own ignorance or by omission, just as there are errors that appear from time to time in AI output. Please remember that we are not your attorney, counselor, investment advisor, or tax advisor. Our mission is to help you understand the powerful tool of artificial intelligence and inspire you to use it for good purposes—lifting burdens, streamlining routine tasks, and elevating mankind and civilization. We hope that you harness the superpower that can come from being a wise AI Whisperer and leverage the power of AI for good.

So, dear reader, here are 50 Ways that you can use ChatGPT to improve your business function, processes, and performance. We will go through each individually, chapter by chapter, as well so you can start to get a clear idea of how to use this innovative tool:

1. Drafting and editing marketing copy
2. Social media content creation
3. Blog post and article generation
4. Email and newsletter templates
5. Writing press releases
6. FAQ sections for websites
7. Product descriptions for online stores
8. Research assistance and fact checking
9. Online chatbot assistance
10. Social media management
11. Content curation
12. Product development and improvement
13. Human resources and recruitment
14. Sales enablement
15. Project management assistance
16. Training and development
17. Internal communications
18. Customer support and service
19. Drafting standard operating procedures (SOPs)
20. Marketing research and competitor analysis
21. Product development and ideation

22. Translating content to different languages
23. Event planning and promotion
24. Sales scripts and training
25. Financial planning and analysis
26. Supply chain and logistics organization
27. Writing and editing business reports
28. Content optimization for SEO
29. Writing business proposals and RFP responses
30. Summarizing lengthy documents
31. Data visualization and reporting
32. Creating engaging presentations
33. Draft external communications
34. Personalizing customer interactions
35. Process improvement and optimization
36. Writing case studies and success stories
37. Managing content calendars and editorial plans
38. Developing creative advertising concepts
39. Sales strategy and pipeline management
40. Brainstorming ideas and solutions
41. ChatGPT as an MS Excel Workbook terminal
42. JavaScript Console
43. Python Script Coder
44. Business Process API Connector
45. Legacy Machines and IoT Integration
46. Solving Employee Engagement Problems
47. Enhancing brand storytelling
48. Developing a Marketing Plan
49. Launching a New Business
50. Selling a Business

These applications of AI and ChatGPT can help small to medium-sized businesses streamline operations, improve communication, enhance marketing efforts, and provide better customer support, ultimately improving overall performance.

From here, let's dive deep into the details of each of these 50 practical uses so you can know exactly how to leverage AI for your company.

Are you excited?

You should be!

Effective Prompts to Get the Best Results from Conversational AI

Now that you have ideas for 50 different ways AI can help your business, before we go through each of them in detail, we wanted to give you a deeper sense of how to get the best quality responses from your AI. If you give the platforms good information, you'll get good information in return. It's a bit of an artform, but we're here to help!

When people get stumped using AI like ChatGPT and other tools, it's important to adjust the approach to improve communication and collaboration between the user and the AI. Here are 25 tips for developing question stems or prompts that help AI understand the user's intent and co-create a valuable conversation and result:

1. Be specific: Clearly define the topic, context, or issue you want the AI to address. Avoid vague or ambiguous questions that can lead to irrelevant or confusing responses.
2. Break it down: If your query is complex or multifaceted, break it down into smaller, more manageable questions. This can help the AI focus on each aspect and provide more accurate and relevant answers.

3. Provide examples: Offer samples or scenarios to illustrate your point or question. This can help the AI grasp the context and deliver more targeted responses.

4. Ask for step-by-step guidance: Instead of asking for a solution or answer outright, request a step-by-step approach or process that the AI can use to address the issue or question.

5. Use keywords: Incorporate relevant keywords or phrases in your prompts to guide the AI's understanding of your query. This can help the AI focus on the most important aspects of your question.

6. Request multiple perspectives: If you want a more comprehensive response, ask the AI to provide multiple perspectives, opinions, or approaches to address the issue or question.

7. Encourage creativity: If you're looking for creative input, explicitly ask the AI to think outside the box or generate unique ideas and solutions.

8. Set limitations: If you have specific constraints or requirements, clearly state them in your prompt to guide the AI's response and ensure it remains within your desired parameters.

9. Ask for clarification: If the AI's response is unclear or confusing, ask for clarification or further explanation to ensure you fully understand the answer provided.

10. Iterate and refine: If the AI's response is not what you were looking for, rephrase your question or provide additional context and information to help the AI better understand your intent.

11. Prioritize your questions: Start with the most important or urgent question to focus the AI's attention on the most critical aspect of your query.

12. Use clear language: Avoid using jargon, slang, or overly complex language when asking your questions. Using simple and direct language can help the AI better understand your intent.

13. Request elaboration: If you need more information on a specific point, ask the AI to elaborate or provide more details.

14. Ask for examples or analogies: Request examples or analogies to help clarify complex concepts or ideas, making them more relatable and understandable.

15. Request a summary: If the AI's response is too lengthy or detailed, ask for a summary or a simplified version of the information.

16. Specify the format: If you have a preference for how the information should be presented (e.g., bullet points, paragraphs, numbered lists), specify the format in your prompt.

17. Verify facts and assumptions: If the AI provides information or makes assumptions that you're unsure about, ask the AI to verify its sources or clarify its assumptions.

18. Use open-ended questions: Encourage the AI to think critically and explore different possibilities by asking open-ended questions that don't have a single correct answer.

19. Ask for pros and cons: Request a balanced perspective by asking the AI to provide both the advantages and disadvantages of a given solution, idea, or approach.

20. Request comparisons: Ask the AI to compare different options, solutions, or approaches to help you make more informed decisions.

21. Encourage reflection: Ask the AI to reflect on its previous responses, considering whether there's any additional information or insights it can offer.
22. Adjust the level of detail: If you need more in-depth information or a higher-level overview, specify the desired level of detail in your prompt.
23. Request a different perspective: If the AI's response is biased or one-sided, ask for an alternative viewpoint or perspective to provide a more balanced understanding.
24. Set a time frame: Specify a time frame for the information or solution you're seeking, which can help the AI provide more relevant and timely responses.
25. Be patient and persistent: Remember that effective communication with ChatGPT can take time and multiple attempts. Be patient and persistent in refining your questions and prompts to achieve the desired outcome.

By applying these strategies, you can enhance your interaction with ChatGPT and maximize the value of the conversation and results.

To go deeper still, we encourage the reader to pick an AI chat response that interests them from the initial question asked of AI, and then go deeper to mine information in that specific vein.

To help the artificial intelligence uncover more data relationships and value, you might consider the following strategies for deeper work:

1. Provide more context: Offer background information, specific details, or relevant data points that can help the AI better understand the scope and intricacies of your query.

2. Ask targeted questions: Focus on specific aspects of the topic, asking the AI to explore particular relationships, correlations, or patterns in the data.

3. Request a multi-layered analysis: Ask the AI to analyze the data from different angles or perspectives, considering numerous dimensions and factors that may influence the relationships between data points.

4. Encourage data visualization: Request the AI to suggest data visualization techniques, such as charts or graphs, that can help reveal hidden patterns, trends, or connections in the data.

5. Combine data sets: If applicable, ask the AI to consider multiple data sets and explore potential relationships or insights that emerge when the data is combined.

6. Use advanced analytical techniques: Encourage the AI to apply machine learning algorithms or statistical models, to uncover deeper relationships in the data.

7. Investigate causality: Ask the artificial intelligence to explore possible causal relationships between variables, considering potential factors that might drive or influence the observed data patterns.

8. Explore outliers: Request the AI to examine variants or unusual data points, considering the factors that may contribute to their deviation from the norm.

9. Look for temporal patterns: Encourage the AI to analyze the data over time, exploring trends, seasonality, or other time-dependent patterns.

10. Consider external factors: Ask the AI to take into account external factors, such as economic, social, or environmental influences, that might impact the data relationships.

11. Examine subgroups: Request the AI to analyze the data by different subgroups or segments, exploring potential variations or disparities within the data.

12. Explore predictive relationships: Encourage the AI to investigate variables that may be useful in forecasting future outcomes or trends.

13. Validate findings: Ask the AI to verify its conclusions by cross-referencing with other data sources or exploring potential biases and limitations in the data.

14. Request actionable insights: Encourage the AI to translate its findings into actionable insights or recommendations that can help you derive value from the data relationships.

15. Iterate and refine: Continuously refine your questions and prompts, building on the AI's previous responses to deepen its analysis and uncover more data relationships and value.

The above questions focus on what you might already know about a topic. Now to go deeper still, consider asking what AI knows that you or other humans do not know. The answer to this type of prompt truly gives you the superpower as AI Whisperers. This will help you lean into a topic and go even deeper.

You might also ask AI what common practices (in your field or topic) humans use that are not evidence-based. Then have AI suggest approaches for evidence-based methods, or ideation that humans have not thought of yet.

If you want deeper insight threads, you could lean into this approach further and ask the following questions to go deeper still:

1. Question assumptions: Ask ChatGPT to challenge common beliefs in a particular field and provide evidence-based alternatives or new perspectives.

2. Explore unconventional ideas: Encourage the AI to generate eccentric or novel ideas that deviate from traditional thinking or practices. From there, evaluate their potential merits and shortcomings.

3. Compare historical and current practices: Request the AI analyze how historical practices have evolved over time and identify any gaps or areas for improvement in current methodologies.

4. Investigate the success of alternative approaches: Ask the AI to research and analyze different methods used in other industries, cultures, or contexts, and assess their potential applicability and effectiveness in your business.

5. Identify cognitive biases: Request the AI to explore common intellectual prejudices or logical fallacies that may influence human decision-making. Suggest ways to mitigate these biases with evidence-based approaches.

6. Analyze contradictory evidence: Encourage the AI to examine conflicting viewpoints on a given topic, and synthesize a balanced perspective based on the available data.

7. Leverage interdisciplinary insights: Ask the AI to draw upon knowledge from different disciplines to generate new ideas, perspectives, or approaches that may not be widely considered within a specific field.

8. Focus on underexplored areas: Request the AI to identify overlooked areas in a particular domain and suggest potential avenues for further research.

9. Evaluate the effectiveness of current practices: Encourage the AI to assess the effectiveness of widely accepted practices, comparing them with alternative methods and highlighting any potential shortcomings or opportunities for improvement.

10. Consider long-term implications: Ask the AI to analyze the consequences of current practices over the next decade or more, identifying potential risks, challenges, or opportunities that may be overlooked in short-term decision-making.

11. Explore the role of technology: Request the AI to investigate how emerging technologies can be leveraged to improve existing practices, create new opportunities, or challenge conventional wisdom.

12. Assess ethical considerations: Encourage the AI to examine the ethical implications of current methods and suggest evidence-based approaches that prioritize ethical concerns or minimize potential harm.

13. Reevaluate priorities and values: Ask the AI to consider whether current standards within a specific domain align with evidence-based practices and suggest potential adjustments or shifts in focus.

14. Investigate the impact of external factors: Request the AI to analyze how influences such as societal, economic, or environmental, may impact current practices and identify evidence-based strategies for adaptation or mitigation.

15. Foster a culture of curiosity: Encourage the AI to maintain a curious and open-minded approach, continuously questioning conventional wisdom and seeking new insights, perspectives, and evidence-based practices.

Finally, as a Chat Whisperer, you always have one more curiosity-engaging final question: "What haven't I asked?" Try using the following prompt structures to explore this line of querying with AI to see what it knows that you don't know:

1. Regarding [topic], can you suggest a question that I might not have thought of asking?
2. What is an important question about [topic] that I haven't considered yet?
3. Please generate a thought-provoking question related to [topic] that I may have overlooked.
4. Can you think of a unique or unexpected question that would encourage deeper exploration of [topic]?
5. What's a question about [topic] that would reveal new insights or perspectives that I haven't considered?

By using these prompt structures, you can encourage the AI to generate questions that help you explore a topic more deeply and consider aspects that you may not have thought of initially.

All these tools will help you become a true AI Whisperer who understands how to leverage artificial intelligence to the fullest.

Now that you know how to go deeper, let's delve into all 50 potential uses of AI that will help your company not only take advantage of this amazing tool, but evolve in ways that will lead you into the next era of business.

Use Case 1:

Drafting and Editing Marketing Copy

One of the best ways to use ChatGPT is to create persuasive, engaging, and targeted marketing copy for all kinds of channels. This doesn't eliminate the need for a human editor, but it will create numerous different versions of text that allows you to save time and foster fresh ideas for websites, social media, emails, and advertisements. AI can help in refining the message, and tailoring content for specific audiences.

Here are 10 potential prompt threads that will get you started using AI in your copy:

1. Suggest 5 headlines for an email campaign promoting our new product.
2. Write a catchy tagline for our upcoming sales event.
3. Create a short, engaging product description for an online store listing.
4. Help me draft copy for a Facebook ad featuring our latest service offering.
5. Write an introduction paragraph for a blog post on the benefits of our product.
6. Suggest ways to improve this existing marketing copy for clarity and impact.
7. Provide 3 call-to-action phrases for a landing page.
8. Generate several key selling points for our product/service.

9. Write a promotional tweet for our upcoming webinar.
10. Help me create an attention-grabbing subject line for our newsletter.

A word of caution here: when asking for marketing copy, make your prompts specific and clear to obtain more relevant and targeted results. If you receive unsatisfactory responses, consider providing more context or adjusting the phrasing of your question. Remember, the better the copy you put in, the better copy you will get out. You can't write first-grade level questions as your prompts and expect the AI to give you Shakespeare.

Use these examples as templates for exploring the remaining use cases. Adapt the synopsis, potential prompts, cautions, and resources to suit each specific application. This will provide a comprehensive resource for users looking to understand and effectively utilize ChatGPT across a wide range of business scenarios.

Further Resources:

1. "Copywriting Secrets" by Jim Edwards - Book on crafting compelling marketing copy.
2. Copyblogger (https://www.copyblogger.com/) - Blog with tips, articles, and resources on content marketing and copywriting.
3. AWAI (https://www.awai.com/) - American Writers & Artists Institute offers courses and resources on copywriting and content creation.
4. HubSpot (https://blog.hubspot.com/marketing/copywriting-101-content-principles-ht) - Marketing blog with numerous articles on copywriting best practices.

Use Case 2:

Social Media Content Creation

Use ChatGPT and create better and more engaging posts for Facebook, Instagram, Twitter, TikTok, LinkedIn, WhatsApp…on and on and on. If you want to make a splash on social media, no matter which platforms work best for your business, content is king. That's a lot of writing, unless of course you leverage ChatGPT to create engaging and shareable content. AI can help you generate ideas, write captions, and develop content that resonates with your target audience.

Here are 10 potential prompt threads for social media posts:

1. Write a Facebook post to promote our upcoming event.
2. Suggest three LinkedIn post ideas to showcase our company culture.
3. Create five tweet drafts about our latest blog post.
4. Write a compelling Instagram caption for a photo of our new product.
5. Help me come up with a series of social media posts for a week-long campaign.
6. Generate ideas for a Twitter thread about a recent industry trend.
7. Write an engaging LinkedIn article on the importance of our services.
8. Create a short video script for an Instagram Reel or TikTok.

9. Suggest ideas for an interactive Facebook poll.
10. Write a response to a customer review or comment on social media.

Keep in mind, when requesting social media content, specify the platform and any character limits or media requirements to get the best results. Adjust your prompt if the response isn't platform-appropriate or engaging enough.

Further Resources:

1. Social Media Examiner (https://www.socialmediaexaminer.com/) - Resources, tips, and strategies for social media marketing.
2. Buffer Blog (https://buffer.com/resources/) - Offers social media marketing tips and insights.
3. Hootsuite Blog (https://blog.hootsuite.com/) - Provides social media marketing news and best practices.
4. Sprout Social Blog (https://sproutsocial.com/insights/) - Shares insights, trends, and best practices for social media marketing.

Use Case 3:

Blog Post and Article Generation

Use ChatGPT to generate blog posts and articles on various topics related to your business or industry. AI can help you draft engaging, informative content that is well-structured, SEO-friendly, and relevant to your target audience.

Here are 10 potential prompt threads:

1. Write an introductory paragraph for an article on the benefits of our product.
2. Suggest five blog post topics related to our industry.
3. Draft an outline for a how-to guide on using our software.
4. Create a list of subheadings for an article on the latest industry trends.
5. Write a conclusion paragraph summarizing key points from a given article.
6. Help me rewrite this blog post section to make it more engaging and informative.
7. Generate content ideas for a series of blog posts targeting our audience personas.
8. Write an article on the importance of sustainability in our industry.
9. Create an engaging and persuasive opinion piece on a relevant industry topic.
10. Draft a case study featuring a successful customer story.

When requesting blog posts or articles, provide specific information about the topic, target audience, and desired format. If the AI-generated content isn't satisfactory, consider refining your instructions or asking for revisions to improve clarity, accuracy, or relevance.

Further Resources:

1. ProBlogger (https://problogger.com/) - Offers blogging tips, strategies, and resources.
2. Copyblogger (https://www.copyblogger.com/blog/) - Provides insights and tips on content marketing, including blog post creation.
3. Moz Blog (https://moz.com/blog) - Shares SEO tips and best practices, useful for optimizing blog content.
4. "Everybody Writes" by Ann Handley (https://amzn.to/3MILL1q) - Book offering guidance on creating effective and engaging content.

Use Case 4:

Email and Newsletter Templates

Social media is great, but the platform owns your client's information. With an email list, you have been given permission to contact your customers directly and can send out messages to engage with them. ChatGPT and AI platforms can create email and newsletter templates that effectively communicate information, promotions, or news to your subscribers. AI can help you craft attractive subject lines, concise copy, and clear calls-to-action for better open rates and conversions.

Here are 10 potential prompt threads:

1. Write a subject line for our monthly newsletter.
2. Draft an email template for a product launch announcement.
3. Create a welcome email sequence for new subscribers.
4. Help me write a follow-up email to a recent event attendee.
5. Write a promotional email for our upcoming sale.
6. Suggest three email subject lines for a customer feedback survey.
7. Draft a template for a personalized product recommendation email.
8. Write a thank you email for a recent purchase or sign-up.
9. Create an email to inform customers about a change in our terms of service.

10. Write a newsletter highlighting our latest blog posts and company updates.

When requesting email or newsletter templates, be specific about the purpose, audience, and key messaging. If the AI-generated content doesn't sound right, you'll need to rephrase your initial request and try to make things clearer or more concise. The better the language in the initial prompt, the better the response.

Further Resources:

1. Email on Acid (https://www.emailonacid.com/blog/) - Provides email marketing tips and best practices.
2. Really Good Emails (https://reallygoodemails.com/) - Offers a curated collection of email design and content examples.
3. Litmus Blog (https://www.litmus.com/blog/) - Shares email marketing insights, trends, and tips.
4. MailerLite Blog (https://www.mailerlite.com/blog) - Offers email marketing strategies and resources.

Use Case 5:

Writing Press Releases

Press releases are still an excellent way to get the word out through news organizations. You never know when something your company is doing will be interesting to a reporter or station manager, so sending out regular releases is a smart marketing tool. Each press release needs to effectively announce newsworthy events, product launches, or company updates. AI can help you create professional, brief, and attention-grabbing press releases that generate interest from media outlets and your customers.

Here are 10 potential prompt threads:

1. Write a press release announcing our new product launch.
2. Draft a press release for our upcoming charity event.
3. Create a press release announcing a major company milestone or achievement.
4. Help me write a press release about a strategic partnership or collaboration.
5. Write a press release announcing a new executive hire or promotion.
6. Draft a press release for a recent industry award or recognition.
7. Create a press release about an upcoming conference or trade show our company is attending.
8. Write a press release announcing a significant investment or funding round.

9. Draft a press release about a new research study or report related to our industry.
10. Create a press release announcing a new company initiative or campaign.

When requesting press releases, be specific about the announcement and any relevant details. News organizations are going to put an extra level of scrutiny on any releases they choose, partially because the station will likely use much of the release verbatim in their reporting. If the AI-generated content isn't up to snuff, you won't get the attention you're looking for. Remember, always be clear in your initial questions so the AI understands exactly what you want.

Further Resources:

1. "The New Rules of Marketing and PR" by David Meerman Scott (https://amzn.to/3KZtDiJ) - Book on creating effective press releases and marketing materials.
2. PR Daily (https://www.prdaily.com/) - Offers public relations tips, strategies, and resources.
3. Cision Blog (https://www.cision.com/us/blog/) - Shares public relations and media relations insights and tips.
4. Muck Rack Blog (https://muckrack.com/blog) - Provides public relations tips, media relations insights, and industry news.

Use Case 6:

FAQ Sections for Websites

Creating FAQ sections for websites involves generating concise, informative, and clear answers to commonly asked questions about a product or service, aimed at addressing customer queries and concerns. AI can compile and write these sections for you in a few minutes. Again, all you're doing is saving time.

Here are 10 potential prompt threads:

1. Identify the most common questions users may have regarding our website.
2. Organize questions into categories.
3. Write clear and concise answers.
4. Use a conversational tone in responses.
5. Incorporate relevant keywords for SEO.
6. Update FAQs regularly based on user feedback.
7. Create an easily navigable FAQ page.
8. Link to relevant resources for further information.
9. Use AI to generate answers to frequently asked questions.
10. Monitor user interactions with the FAQ section to optimize its effectiveness.

When leveraging AI for FAQ sections, ensure that the AI-generated content is accurate, consistent with your brand voice, and genuinely helpful to users. Always review and edit AI-generated content before publishing.

Further Resources:

1. https://www.helpscout.com/ HelpScout is a customer support software company that provides a suite of tools to help businesses manage their customer interactions. Their website offers a variety of resources for businesses, including blog posts, webinars, and case studies.
2. https://yoast.com/ Yoast is a company that provides SEO software and tools for WordPress websites. Their website offers a variety of resources for WordPress users, including blog posts, tutorials, and guides.

Use Case 7:

Product Descriptions for Online Stores

Writing product descriptions for online stores involves crafting engaging, informative, and persuasive copy that highlights the features and benefits of a product. What you're trying to do is entice potential customers to make a purchase. You can write all these descriptions yourself, or you can let ChatGPT or another artificial intelligence platform do it for you. Yes, you'll still need to edit what the AI came up with, but you'd have to edit what a human wrote too, while waiting a week to get all the content.

Here are 10 potential prompt threads that will allow you to get that online store up and running fast:

1. Identify the target audience and their needs.
2. Highlight the key features and benefits of the product.
3. Use descriptive language to create a vivid mental image.
4. Maintain a consistent brand voice.
5. Incorporate relevant keywords for SEO.
6. Include technical specifications where necessary.
7. Address potential objections or concerns.
8. Use AI to generate product descriptions based on input data.
9. Test different copy variations to optimize conversion rates.
10. Regularly update product descriptions as needed.

Again, always edit whatever the AI comes up with. Sometimes content can get a bit wonky, but with a human eye, and a simple refresh on the prompts you're giving the program, the information that the AI will provide is pretty amazing.

Further Resources:

1. https://www.shopify.com/blog/8211159-9-simple-ways-to-write-product-descriptions-that-sell
2. https://www.bigcommerce.com/ BigCommerce is a cloud-based ecommerce platform that allows businesses to create, manage, and grow their online stores. The platform offers a variety of features and tools.

Use Case 8:

Research Assistance and Fact-Checking

Don't you love research tasks and fact-checking?

No?

Well, very few people do, and even fewer can do it at the speed of business. AI is incredible at providing summaries, key information, or data points from a variety of sources. AI can help save time by delivering quick insights and verifying the accuracy of information.

Here are 10 potential prompt threads:

1. Provide a summary of the latest trends in our industry.
2. Fact-check the claim that our product reduces energy consumption by 30%.
3. Research and summarize the key features of our competitor's new product.
4. Find three statistics on the growth of the e-commerce market in the past five years.
5. Verify the accuracy of a quote attributed to a famous entrepreneur.
6. Provide a list of the top five industry conferences to attend this year.
7. Research and summarize the potential impact of new regulations on our business.

8. Identify the main competitors in our market and their unique selling points.
9. Find and summarize customer reviews or testimonials for our product.
10. Research and report on the effectiveness of a specific marketing strategy in our industry.

When requesting research assistance or fact-checking, don't leave out any details. And keep in mind that ChatGPT's knowledge is up-to-date only through September 2021. If the AI-generated information is outdated, incomplete, or inaccurate, consider conducting further research using reliable sources. These are great instances to use Google Bard and MS Bing Chat that are connected to the internet. Just like with a human fact-checker, you'll need to go through and make sure all sources are current and reputable.

Further Resources:

1. Statista (https://www.statista.com/) - Provides access to statistics, market data, and industry insights.
2. Google Scholar (https://scholar.google.com/) - Offers a search engine for scholarly literature, including articles, books, and conference papers.
3. World Bank Open Data (https://data.worldbank.org/) - Offers a comprehensive source of global development data.
4. FactCheck.org (https://www.factcheck.org/) - A non-partisan fact-checking website that verifies the accuracy of statements and claims.

Use Case 9:

Online Chatbot Support Assistance

Implement ChatGPT to enhance your customer support operations by providing quick and accurate responses to frequently asked questions, troubleshooting common issues, or guiding customers through self-help resources. AI can help improve response times, reduce support costs, and increase customer satisfaction.

This time we're giving you 20 potential prompt threads, so get ready:

1. How do I set up my new account on your platform?
2. What is the return policy for your products?
3. How do I reset my password if I've forgotten it?
4. Can you provide instructions for assembling your product?
5. What are the key features of your service plan?
6. How do I contact customer support for further assistance?
7. Can I change my order after it's been placed?
8. What are your shipping options and estimated delivery times?
9. How do I apply a promo code to my purchase?
10. Are there any known compatibility issues with your software?
11. Provide a step-by-step solution for resetting a user's password.

12. Explain the process of upgrading to a premium subscription.
13. Address a customer's concerns about data privacy and security.
14. Troubleshoot a common issue with our software installation.
15. Guide a customer through setting up their new account.
16. Explain the benefits and features of our product to a potential customer.
17. Offer tips for optimizing the use of our product or service.
18. Provide assistance with processing a return or refund request.
19. Respond to a customer inquiry about billing or payment issues.
20. Offer a detailed comparison between two of our product offerings.

Ensure that the AI chatbot has an up-to-date knowledge base and can accurately address customer inquiries. Monitor interactions to ensure the chatbot provides appropriate information. Also, be prepared to redirect customers to human support when necessary.

Further Resources:

1. Chatbot Magazine (https://chatbotsmagazine.com/) - Offers news, insights, and tips for chatbot development.
2. MobileMonkey (https://mobilemonkey.com/blog) - Blog with resources on chatbot marketing and development.
3. Drift Blog (https://www.drift.com/blog/) - Shares insights, tips, and strategies for conversational marketing, including chatbot development.

4. Chatbot Tutorials (https://chatbotslife.com/) - A resource for chatbot developers, featuring tutorials, news, and insights.
5. Zendesk (https://www.zendesk.com/) - Offers customer support software and resources.
6. Freshdesk (https://freshdesk.com/) - Provides a customer support platform and resources.
7. Help Scout (https://www.helpscout.com/) - Offers customer support software and resources.
8. "The Effortless Experience" by Matthew Dixon, Nick Toman, and Rick DeLisi (https://amzn.to/41bSHsC) - Book on providing exceptional customer support and reducing customer effort.

Use Case 10:

Social Media Management

Social media is in a constant state of flux. What worked to get traction on posts and ads six months ago likely doesn't work today. Utilize ChatGPT to manage your company's social media presence, from generating engaging content and post ideas to crafting compelling captions, hashtags, and responses to comments or messages. This is one thing AI can stay on top of since it can see the overarching patterns we can't. It will save time, maintain a consistent posting schedule, and increase audience engagement.

Since this is such a big subject, we decided to give you 20 powerful questions to ask AI for your social media management:

1. Write an engaging caption for our latest product release announcement on Instagram.
2. Suggest five Twitter post ideas related to our industry.
3. Draft a LinkedIn post highlighting our recent company achievement.
4. Create a series of Facebook post ideas for our upcoming event or promotion.
5. Help me respond to a customer inquiry or comment on social media.
6. Generate a list of relevant hashtags for our Instagram campaign.
7. Write a social media post announcing a new blog article on our website.

8. Create a series of engaging questions or polls for our audience on Twitter.
9. Draft a LinkedIn post promoting a job opening at our company.
10. Write a social media post celebrating a company milestone or anniversary.
11. Write a social media post to promote our latest product launch.
12. Develop a list of hashtag suggestions for our industry or niche.
13. Suggest strategies for increasing engagement on our Instagram account.
14. Create a series of tweet ideas to showcase our company culture.
15. Write a LinkedIn post highlighting company insights.
16. Develop a monthly social media content calendar.
17. Suggest potential collaborations or partnerships for social media campaigns.
18. Write a Facebook post sharing insights and polling customer prospects.
19. Create a list of social media post ideas focused on customer success stories.
20. Write a social media caption for a behind-the-scenes photo of our team.

When requesting social media management assistance from an AI, provide specific information about the platform, desired tone, and content objectives. Twitter is different from Facebook, which is different from LinkedIn. A post on one won't necessarily be appropriate or functional on another platform. If the AI-generated content is unsatisfactory or off-brand, consider refining your prompt or asking for revisions to better align with your company's voice and goals.

Further Resources:

1. Hootsuite Blog (https://blog.hootsuite.com/) - Offers social media management tips and resources.
2. Sprout Social Blog (https://sproutsocial.com/insights/) - Shares insights and best practices on social media marketing.
3. Buffer Blog (https://buffer.com/resources/) - Provides social media marketing tips and resources.
4. "Jab, Jab, Jab, Right Hook" by Gary Vaynerchuk (https://amzn.to/3MOKNRD) - Book on creating effective social media content.

Use Case 11:

Content Curation

Content is king.

Good content, that is.

Still, you need to engage your audience, and leveraging ChatGPT to curate relevant and engaging content for your audience is a great way to do it. You can create industry news, articles, videos, or podcasts. AI can help save time by identifying and summarizing valuable content that aligns with your company's interests and target audience, fostering engagement and thought leadership.

10 Potential Prompt Threads:

1. Find and summarize three recent articles about the latest trends in our industry.
2. Curate a list of five relevant podcasts for our audience.
3. Identify and summarize the key takeaways from a popular industry report.
4. Recommend five YouTube channels that provide valuable content for our niche.
5. Curate a list of influential industry leaders or experts to follow on social media.
6. Find and summarize recent news articles related to our product or service.

7. Suggest three relevant industry conferences or events for our team to attend.
8. Identify five must-read books for professionals in our field.
9. Curate a list of insightful blog posts related to a specific topic in our industry.
10. Find and summarize recent research studies or whitepapers in our field.

When requesting content curation assistance from an AI, provide specific information about your industry, niche, and audience preferences. If the AI-generated content is not relevant or valuable, consider refining your prompt or providing additional context to better align with your target audience's interests.

Further Resources:

1. Feedly (https://feedly.com/) - Offers a content curation tool to discover and organize industry news, blogs, and publications.
2. Pocket (https://getpocket.com/) - Provides a platform for saving and curating articles, videos, and other content from the web.
3. "The Content Trap" by Bharat Anand (https://amzn.to/43z4OBj) - Book on the strategic importance of content in the digital age.
4. Content Marketing Institute (https://contentmarketinginstitute.com/) - Offers resources and insights on content marketing and curation.

Use Case 12:

Product Development and Improvement

Utilize ChatGPT to assist in product development and improvement by generating ideas for new features, enhancements, or potential problem areas to address. AI can help foster innovation, improve product-market fit, and maintain a competitive edge in the market.

10 Potential Prompt Threads:

1. Suggest five potential new features for our software platform.
2. Identify areas of improvement for our mobile app's user experience.
3. Brainstorm ways to increase the energy efficiency of our product.
4. Suggest potential integrations or partnerships to enhance our product's capabilities.
5. Generate ideas for expanding our product line to target new customer segments.
6. Help evaluate the pros and cons of a specific product feature.
7. Identify and address potential usability issues in our product design.
8. Brainstorm ways to improve our product's packaging or presentation.

9. Suggest potential improvements to our product's onboarding process.
10. Evaluate our product against competitor offerings and suggest areas for improvement.

There are a lot of nuances when it comes to product development, but AI will allow you to process a lot of ideas quickly. You're more likely to find something worthwhile from 1,000 concepts versus only 100. That's what AI will allow you to do. As always, when requesting product development and improvement assistance, provide specific information about your product and what you want that product to accomplish. Ask detailed questions, and you're likely to achieve better results.

Further Resources:

1. Mind the Product (https://www.mindtheproduct.com/) - Offers resources and insights on product management and development.
2. "Inspired: How to Create Tech Products Customers Love" by Marty Cagan - Book on product management and development best practices.
3. Product Hunt (https://www.producthunt.com/) - Provides a platform for discovering and showcasing new products and features.
4. "The Lean Startup" by Eric Ries (https://amzn.to/41kkyX8) - Book on creating and managing successful startups and product development.

Use Case 13:

Human Resources and Recruitment

Algorithms do a better job of choosing potential hires than humans do. It's an uncomfortable fact. That being the case, using ChatGPT to streamline human resources and recruitment processes, such as drafting job descriptions, screening resumes, creating interview questions, or developing employee onboarding materials, is a great use of the tool. AI can help save time, improve candidate experience, and ensure a more efficient hiring process.

Here are 10 prompt threads that will help you hire superior executives and sales personnel:

1. Write a compelling job description for a software engineer position.
2. Suggest five interview questions to assess a candidate's problem-solving skills.
3. Create an onboarding checklist for new employees.
4. Draft a welcome email for new hires.
5. Identify key skills and qualifications in a candidate's resume.
6. Write a rejection email for unsuccessful job applicants.
7. Suggest potential improvements to our employee training program.
8. Create a list of team-building activities for remote employees.

9. Help develop a survey to gather employee feedback on company culture.
10. Suggest strategies for promoting diversity and inclusion in our hiring process.

Human resources and recruitment can be very personal aspects of your business, so always make sure to edit and verify all correspondence have the proper tone. This is of course something you would want to do even if you weren't using AI. Provide specific information about the role, company culture, and desired outcomes for all job opening posts. If the AI-generated content doesn't align with your HR goals, check the questions you asked, and the prompts given to verify what you may have left out.

Further Resources:

1. SHRM (https://www.shrm.org/) - Society for Human Resource Management offers resources and insights on HR best practices.
2. "Work Rules!" by Laszlo Bock (https://amzn.to/3UEV052) - Book on human resources and management strategies at Google.
3. HR Dive (https://www.hrdive.com/) - Provides news, analysis, and resources on human resources trends and best practices.
4. "The Talent Code" by Daniel Coyle (https://amzn.to/41lRChC) - Book on nurturing talent and skill development in organizations.
5. "The Talent Palette" by Severin Sorensen (in press, May 2023). A book about identifying and capturing difference making top talent, and the methods to attract, screen, test, and select them.

Use Case 14:

Sales Enablement

Sales enablement is the set of tools and content you provide your sales team so they can accelerate overall company transactions. You can employ ChatGPT to enhance your sales enablement efforts by generating sales scripts, email templates, objection handling techniques, or product comparisons. AI can help improve sales effectiveness, shorten sales cycles, and increase win rates.

10 Potential Prompt Threads:

1. Write a sales script for cold calling potential clients.
2. Draft a follow-up email template after a sales meeting or presentation.
3. Suggest five techniques for handling common sales objections.
4. Create a comparison chart between our product and a competitor's offering.
5. Write a persuasive sales pitch for our product or service.
6. Develop a set of qualifying questions to identify potential customers.
7. Provide a list of key selling points for our product to use in sales conversations.
8. Draft an email template to re-engage with a prospect who has gone silent.

9. Suggest strategies for building rapport with potential clients.
10. Create a list of success stories or case studies to share with prospects.

When requesting sales enablement assistance, provide specific information about your product, target audience, and sales process. The more details you give the AI platform, the closer the material will be to your requirements. If you get stuck, simply try rephrasing your prompt with a few different words. Something simple like that can completely change the AI's content outcome.

Further Resources:

1. HubSpot Sales Blog (https://blog.hubspot.com/sales) - Offers resources and insights on sales strategies and best practices.
2. "The Challenger Sale" by Matthew Dixon and Brent Adamson (https://amzn.to/3MKyxl4) - Book on sales techniques for complex sales environments.
3. Sales Hacker (https://www.saleshacker.com/) - Provides resources, articles, and webinars on sales enablement and strategies.
4. "SPIN Selling" by Neil Rackham (https://amzn.to/3GJClzg) - Book on a research-based sales approach focused on situation, problem, implication, and need-payoff.

Use Case 15:

Project Management Assistance

Once again, the power of AI truly comes out when dealing with time-consuming tasks that chew up the hours. Generating task lists, schedules, risk assessments, or progress reports should become the prevue of artificial intelligence in your company. AI can help improve project organization, ensure timely completion, and optimize resource allocation.

10 potential prompt threads for project management:

1. Create a task list for launching a new marketing campaign.
2. Develop a project timeline for a website redesign.
3. Identify potential risks and mitigation strategies for a software development project.
4. Write a progress report for a client on the status of their project.
5. Suggest strategies for improving team communication during a project.
6. Provide a list of tools and resources for effective project management.
7. Develop a process for tracking and reporting project milestones.
8. Create a checklist for closing out a completed project.

9. Suggest methods for prioritizing tasks and allocating resources effectively.
10. Identify potential bottlenecks or delays in a project plan.

When requesting project management assistance, provide specific information about the project, goals, and desired outcomes. If the AI-generated content is not relevant or useful, consider refining your prompt or providing additional context to better align with your project management needs.

Further Resources:

1. Project Management Institute (https://www.pmi.org/) - Offers resources, certifications, and insights on project management best practices.
2. "The Lean Startup" by Eric Ries (https://amzn.to/41kkyX8) - Book on creating and managing successful startups and project development.
3. "Making Things Happen" by Scott Berkun (https://amzn.to/3zVuSJz) - Book on project management strategies and techniques.
4. Trello (https://trello.com/) - Provides a project management tool for organizing tasks and tracking progress.

Use Case 16:

Training and Development

Training materials, tutorials, and educational resources for employees, customers, or partners are a key aspect of any business. It is best they meet legal requirements and are clear and concise. AI can help enhance the learning experience, reduce the time required to create training materials, and ensure a more consistent understanding of key concepts. And when it comes to making sure all legal requirements are included to protect your company? AI has you covered.

10 Potential Prompt Threads:

1. Write a tutorial on how to use a specific feature of our software.
2. Develop a training module on effective communication skills.
3. Create a quiz to assess employees' understanding of company policies.
4. Write a user guide for our product, focusing on setup and basic operations.
5. Suggest five interactive activities for a team-building workshop.
6. Develop a training plan for onboarding new employees.
7. Create a list of resources for employees to improve their professional skills.

8. Write a script for a training video on customer service best practices.
9. Develop a training module on diversity and inclusion in the workplace.
10. Write a step-by-step guide for troubleshooting a common issue with our product.

As you can see from the potential prompts we've given, it's easy to make sure you meet all legal requirements in your documents and keep an eye on diversity as well. If your HR professional is up to date on your current industry standards in these areas, it shouldn't be a problem making sure the AI covers all your bases.

Further Resources:

1. Lynda (https://www.lynda.com/) - Offers online courses in a variety of professional skills and topics.
2. "The Fifth Discipline" by Peter Senge (https://amzn.to/3L0yVKQ) - Book on fostering learning organizations and continuous improvement.
3. Training Industry (https://trainingindustry.com/) - Provides resources, insights, and best practices on corporate training and development.
4. "The Adult Learner" by Malcolm Knowles, Elwood Holton, and Richard Swanson (https://amzn.to/4093Etq) - Book on adult learning principles and strategies.

Use Case 17:

Internal Communications

ChatGPT and other AI platforms are perfect tools to enhance internal communications within your organization, such as drafting company announcements, newsletters, meeting agendas, or employee recognition messages. One of the biggest factors is how AI can help improve communication efficiency, maintain a positive work environment, and keep employees informed and engaged.

10 Potential Prompt Threads:

1. Draft a company-wide announcement regarding a new product launch.
2. Create a monthly newsletter highlighting departmental achievements and updates.
3. Write a meeting agenda for an upcoming team retreat.
4. Develop an email recognizing an employee's outstanding performance.
5. Suggest ideas for a regular internal communication series to keep employees informed.
6. Create a list of topics for a company-wide town hall meeting.
7. Write a memo outlining a new company policy or procedure.
8. Develop an email template for sharing project updates with stakeholders.

9. Suggest strategies for improving cross-departmental communication.
10. Write a script for a video message from the CEO to employees.

When requesting internal communications assistance, provide specific information about the context, audience, and what you want the content to accomplish. If the AI-generated scripts aren't applicable or successful, consider retooling your prompt or providing additional context to better align with your company's communication goals. Adapt the synopsis, potential prompts, cautions, and resources to suit each specific application.

Further Resources:

1. Slack (https://slack.com/) - Provides a platform for team communication and collaboration.
2. "Crucial Conversations" by Kerry Patterson, Joseph Grenny, Ron McMillan, and Al Switzler (https://amzn.to/3KXUonJ) - Book on effective communication strategies for high-stakes conversations.
3. Ragan Communications (https://www.ragan.com/) - Offers resources, insights, and best practices on internal communications and employee engagement.
4. "Made to Stick" by Chip Heath and Dan Heath (https://amzn.to/3A2BRAp) - Book on creating memorable and impactful messages.

Use Case 18:

Customer Support and Service

Some of the most successful companies in the world have cornered their respective markets, not being the cheapest, but by offering the best service. Leverage ChatGPT to enhance your own customer service. AI can generate response templates, troubleshooting guides, FAQ content, or customer satisfaction survey materials.

What would improving customer experience and loyalty do for your business?

It's time to find out with 10 triggers to get AI cooking up new ideas:

1. Write a customer service email template addressing a common issue.
2. Develop a troubleshooting guide for a specific product or service.
3. Create a list of frequently asked questions (FAQs) and their answers.
4. Write a follow-up email to a customer after resolving their issue.
5. Suggest strategies for improving customer satisfaction and loyalty.
6. Develop a list of potential customer service performance metrics.

7. Create a customer satisfaction survey to gather feedback on our support efforts.
8. Write a knowledge base article explaining a complex product feature.
9. Develop a list of potential customer service training topics or resources.
10. Suggest best practices for handling difficult or escalated customer situations.

For the best customer service and support assistance ideas, be specific with who your customers are already. If you're a transport company, new customers aren't going to come from a segment of the population that has no need to transport material. Give AI the details it needs to provide you with the results you want. Specificity is king!

Further Resources:

1. "The Effortless Experience" by Matthew Dixon, Nick Toman, and Rick DeLisi (https://amzn.to/3UJQQsr) - Book on delivering exceptional customer service.
2. Customer Think (https://customerthink.com/) - Offers resources, insights, and best practices on customer service and experience.
3. "Delivering Happiness" by Tony Hsieh (https://amzn.to/3mt1K9v) - Book on building a customer-centric company culture.
4. Help Scout (https://www.helpscout.com/) - Provides resources, insights, and best practices on customer service and support.

Use Case 19:

Drafting Standard Operating Procedures (SOPs)

Anyone out there absolutely love drafting standard operating procedures that outline step-by-step processes for various tasks within your organization? We're willing to bet there are very few hands raised right now. Let ChatGPT help you create clear, concise, and easy-to-follow instructions that ensure consistency, compliance, and efficiency across your team.

10 Potential Prompt Threads:

1. Write an SOP for processing customer refunds.
2. Create a step-by-step guide for onboarding new employees.
3. Develop an SOP for handling customer complaints.
4. Provide instructions for conducting routine equipment maintenance.
5. Outline the process for submitting expense reports within the company.
6. Draft an SOP for conducting regular inventory checks.
7. Describe the steps for escalating technical issues to the IT department.
8. Write an SOP for updating the company's social media accounts.
9. Create guidelines for approving and publishing blog posts.

10. Develop a procedure for organizing and archiving important documents.

When requesting SOPs, be specific about the process and any unique requirements or compliance standards. From there, your HR specialist will need to ensure the AI-generated SOP is accurate, clear, and comprehensive. Review and revise the content as needed to guarantee it meets your organization's standards and expectations.

Further Resources:

1. Process Street (https://www.process.st/) - A platform for creating and managing SOPs, checklists, and workflows.
2. SweetProcess (https://www.sweetprocess.com/) - Offers tools and resources for documenting and managing standard operating procedures.
3. Tallyfy (https://tallyfy.com/) - A workflow and process management software with a focus on SOPs.
4. "Effective SOPs: Make Your Standard Operating Procedures Help Your Business Become More Productive" by Giles Johnston (https://amzn.to/40cA5Hv)

Use Case 20:

Market Research and Competitor Analysis

Employ ChatGPT to support market research and analysis efforts by generating competitor analyses, identifying industry trends, summarizing market reports, or brainstorming product or service improvement ideas. Imagine the wealth of documentation and investigation an AI can do in a matter of minutes, providing you with a broad look at your industry or financial markets in general. Your ability to make informed decisions will be enhanced, allowing you to identify more opportunities, and maintain your competitive edge.

Let's dive into 10 prompts that will allow you to dominate your market:

1. Conduct a competitor analysis for our main competitors in the market.
2. Identify emerging trends in our industry and potential implications for our business.
3. Summarize key findings from a recent market research report.
4. Develop a list of potential improvements for our product based on customer feedback.
5. Suggest strategies for entering a new market segment or geographic region.
6. Write a SWOT analysis (Strengths, Weaknesses, Opportunities, Threats) for our company.

7. Identify potential partnerships or collaborations that could benefit our business.
8. Analyze the effectiveness of our current pricing strategy and suggest improvements.
9. Develop a list of potential new features or services based on market trends.
10. Write a report on the potential impact of new regulations or policies on our industry.

Read prompt #10 again. Imagine having an up-to-date understanding of government policy and regulation on your business.

That is huge!

As always, if the AI-generated content isn't relevant or effective, consider refining your prompt or providing additional context to better align with your research goals.

Further Resources:

1. Statista (https://www.statista.com/) - Offers a wide range of statistics and market data across various industries.
2. "Blue Ocean Strategy" by W. Chan Kim and Renée Mauborgne (https://amzn.to/3L2mePR) - Book on identifying and capitalizing on uncontested market spaces.
3. MarketResearch.com (https://www.marketresearch.com/) - Provides access to market research reports and industry analysis.
4. "The Innovator's Dilemma" by Clayton M. Christensen (https://amzn.to/3GGnxkI) - Book on disruptive innovation and its impact on established markets.

Use Case 21:

Product Development and Ideation

Employees with great ideas, who can then implement them, are a huge asset to any business. They are integral to your success. Where AI can amplify this is in its ability to generate large numbers of ideas for new products and services. By harnessing the power of ChatGPT to support product development and ideation efforts, you will generate hundreds of new product ideas, feature suggestions, or product improvement ideas based on market trends, customer feedback, or competitive landscape. AI can help inspire innovation, streamline development, and enhance customer satisfaction.

10 potential prompt threads for generating new ideas:

1. Brainstorm new product ideas for our company within our industry.
2. Suggest innovative features to add to our existing product line.
3. Identify areas of improvement for our current products based on customer feedback.
4. Analyze market trends and suggest potential product opportunities.
5. Develop a list of potential product names and descriptions for a new offering.
6. Write a pitch for a new product idea targeting a specific customer segment.

7. Suggest ways to enhance the user experience of our product.
8. Conduct a competitor analysis to identify gaps in their product offerings.
9. Brainstorm ideas for a new product line extension.
10. Suggest strategies for incorporating sustainability or eco-friendliness into our products.

When requesting product development and ideation assistance, provide specific information about your industry, market, and company goals. Refine your prompt or provide clearer context if you find the ideas aren't detailed or focused enough on your particular industry.

Further Resources:

1. "Hooked" by Nir Eyal (https://amzn.to/3zWFp78) - Book on creating habit-forming products.
2. Product Hunt (https://www.producthunt.com/) - Showcases new products and innovations.
3. "The Lean Product Playbook" by Dan Olsen (https://amzn.to/3L1cZPS) - Book on product development and management techniques.
4. Mind the Product (https://www.mindtheproduct.com/) - Provides resources, insights, and best practices on product management and development.

Use Case 22:

Translating Content to Different Languages

Translating content to different languages involves converting text from one language to another while preserving the meaning, tone, and context of the original content. If you have a multinational corporation, translations become incredibly important. You want to ensure that your documents, website, and social media messages are accessible and understandable to a global audience.

ChatGPT and other AI platforms have become incredibly skilled at translating from one language to another. These programs have access to millions of documents and can readily convert content for audiences all around the globe.

If you want to take advantage of this tool, here are 10 steps that will make sure you're doing it right:

1. Identify the target languages and audiences.
2. Understand cultural nuances and linguistic differences; for example, you can ask it to translate a word, phrase, or article into another language with a specific dialect: e.g., Spanish, using Cubano style.
3. Preserve the meaning and context of the original content.
4. Adapt content to accommodate language-specific idioms and expressions.
5. Use AI-powered translation tools, such as machine translation, for initial translations.

6. Edit and proofread translated content for accuracy and readability.
7. Collaborate with native speakers or professional translators for quality assurance.
8. Optimize translated content for SEO in target languages.
9. Monitor and analyze the performance of translated content.
10. Continuously update and improve translated content based on feedback.

When using AI for translating content, be aware that machine translations may not always accurately convey the nuances, tone, or context of the original content. So much of language comes down to context and turn of phrase. Don't lose sight of that and assume your meaning is coming across. Always work with native speakers or professional translators to review and edit AI-generated translations. The last thing you want to do is offend a segment of your audience merely because you made a direct translation without paying attention to how those specific phrases would be interpreted by your customers.

Further Resources:

1. https://www.deepl.com/translator - DeepL Translate is a machine translation service that offers high-quality translations in over 26 languages. It is known for its accuracy and fluency, and it is often considered to be one of the best machine translation services available.
2. https://translate.google.com/ - Google Translate is another popular machine translation service that offers translations in over 100 languages. It is known for its ease of use and its wide

range of features, such as the ability to translate text, speech, and documents.

Use Case 23

Event Planning and Promotion

Depending on your business, event planning and promotion efforts can be a huge part of revenue generation. Community and customer outreach are another way AI can make life easier by generating event ideas, promotional materials, agendas, or post-event follow-up content. AI can help ensure a successful event, increase attendee engagement, and streamline the planning process. All the initial work will be done quickly and effectively without much effort from any particular employee. Their time can then be spent on more important tasks.

Need to plan that next big advertising event? Here are 10 triggers that will get AI moving in the right direction:

1. Brainstorm ideas for a unique company event or team-building activity.
2. Write a promotional email for an upcoming industry conference.
3. Develop an event agenda, including keynote speakers and breakout sessions.
4. Create a social media campaign to promote an upcoming event.
5. Write a post-event summary to share with attendees and non-attendees.
6. Suggest strategies for increasing event attendance and engagement.

7. Develop a list of potential sponsors or partners for our event.
8. Write a press release announcing an upcoming event or conference.
9. Create a list of tips for attendees to make the most of our event.
10. Write a follow-up email to attendees, thanking them for their participation and requesting feedback.

When requesting event planning and promotion assistance, always look to your target audience, and what you need the event to accomplish. If you're focused on customer retention, you'll want to make that the emphasis of the information you feed the AI. And if you don't know what the goal of the event or promotion should be, feel free to ask the AI for help with that too. The AI won't judge.

Further Resources:

1. "The Art of Gathering" by Priya Parker (https://amzn.to/3GIb4Ni) - Book on creating transformative events and experiences.
2. Eventbrite (https://www.eventbrite.com/) - Offers a platform for creating, promoting, and managing events.
3. "Event Planning: The Ultimate Guide" by Judy Allen (https://amzn.to/3mxfVu7) - Comprehensive guide to event planning and management.
4. BizBash (https://www.bizbash.com/) - Provides resources, insights, and best practices on event planning and promotion.

Use Case 24:

Sales Scripts and Training

Use ChatGPT to enhance your sales enablement and training efforts by creating sales scripts, objection handling guides, product positioning materials, or training resources for your sales team. Sales performance will improve, revenues will increase, and a more consistent sales process will be ensured. It's all just a few smart prompts away from being reality!

And here are 10 that will get your mind moving and AI processing:

1. Write a sales script for a cold call or product pitch.
2. Develop a guide for handling common sales objections.
3. Create a product comparison chart showcasing our product against competitors.
4. Write an email template for following up with potential leads.
5. Suggest strategies for increasing sales performance and closing deals.
6. Develop a list of potential upselling or cross-selling opportunities.
7. Create a sales training guide for new hires.
8. Write a case study showcasing a successful customer engagement.
9. Develop a list of questions to qualify potential leads effectively.

10. Suggest best practices for building rapport and trust with prospects.

If by now you're not seeing the power of AI, go back and read Number 10 again. How valuable is rapport and trust in your business? If you can strengthen ideals like that in your interactions with clients, it could mean the difference between feeling the pinch of an economic downturn and riding a wave of success despite a recession.

When generating sales enablement and training assistance from AI, provide specific details about your product, target audience, and sales goals. If the AI-generated content is not relevant or effective, refine your prompt or provide additional context so the AI has a better understanding of your needs.

Further Resources:

1. "The Challenger Sale" by Matthew Dixon and Brent Adamson (https://amzn.to/3MKyxl4) - Book on a new approach to selling.
2. Sales Hacker (https://www.saleshacker.com/) - Offers resources, insights, and best practices on sales enablement and training.
3. "SPIN Selling" by Neil Rackham (https://amzn.to/3GJClzg) - Book on a consultative selling approach.
4. HubSpot Sales Blog (https://blog.hubspot.com/sales) - Provides resources, insights, and best practices on sales techniques and strategies.

Use Case 25:

Financial Planning and Analysis

Leverage ChatGPT to support financial planning and analysis efforts by generating budget templates, financial projections, investment strategies, or cost-saving ideas. AI can help improve financial decision-making, identify opportunities for growth, and optimize resource allocation.

10 Potential Prompt Threads:

1. Develop a budget template for a specific department or project.
2. Create a financial projection for our company's revenue and expenses over the next year.
3. Suggest investment strategies for our company's cash reserves.
4. Identify potential cost-saving opportunities within our operations.
5. Write a financial analysis of a recent company acquisition.
6. Develop a list of key performance indicators (KPIs) for tracking financial success.
7. Suggest strategies for optimizing cash flow and working capital.
8. Create a financial risk assessment for a potential new market entry.

9. Develop a capital expenditure plan for our company's expansion efforts.
10. Write a financial summary for our annual report or shareholder presentation.

We're halfway done.

I don't know about you, but the sheer volume of AI services is mind-boggling.

This is what we've been talking about! Imagine having all these services handled quickly, simply by having someone know what prompts to use. It's a business-changer that I hope you're starting to get excited about.

And again, we're only half-done!

Further Resources:

1. "Financial Intelligence for Entrepreneurs" by Karen Berman and Joe Knight (https://amzn.to/3MJ0edO) - Book on understanding and managing business financials.
2. Investopedia (https://www.investopedia.com/) - Offers resources, insights, and best practices on finance, investing, and financial analysis.
3. "The Lean Startup" by Eric Ries (https://amzn.to/41kkyX8) - Book on optimizing resource allocation and financial planning for startups.
4. Corporate Finance Institute (https://corporatefinanceinstitute.com/) - Provides resources, insights, and best practices on corporate finance and financial analysis.

Use Case 26:

Supply Chain and Logistics Optimization

Supply chain issues have been common over the last few years. Efficiencies can take a lot of time to identify and are costly to implement. AI streamlines your logistics efforts by generating process improvement ideas, inventory management strategies, transportation planning, or supplier evaluations. This will improve efficiency, reduce costs, and increase overall supply chain performance.

10 Potential Prompt Threads:

1. Suggest strategies for optimizing our inventory management processes.
2. Identify potential cost-saving opportunities within our supply chain operations.
3. Develop a transportation plan for shipping our products more efficiently.
4. Suggest ways to reduce lead times and improve order fulfillment.
5. Write a supplier evaluation report for a potential new vendor.
6. Develop a list of key performance indicators (KPIs) for tracking supply chain success.

7. Suggest strategies for mitigating supply chain disruptions and risks.
8. Create a contingency plan for dealing with unexpected supply chain challenges.
9. Develop a list of potential alternative suppliers to diversify our supply chain.
10. Write a case study showcasing a successful supply chain optimization effort.

When requesting supply chain and logistics optimization assistance, provide specific information about your company's operations, goals, and what efficiencies you're looking to improve. Play around with the wording of your prompts if you find the information isn't skewing in the direction you need.

Further Resources:

1. "The Supply Chain Revolution" by Suman Sarkar (https://amzn.to/3UBe0RA) - Book on innovative supply chain management practices.
2. Supply Chain Digital (https://www.supplychaindigital.com/) - Offers resources, insights, and best practices on supply chain and logistics optimization.
3. "Lean Supply Chain and Logistics Management" by Paul Myerson (https://amzn.to/3L30raJ) - Book on applying lean principles to supply chain management.
4. Supply Chain Management Review (https://www.scmr.com/) - Provides resources, insights, and best practices on supply chain management and logistics.

Use Case 27:

Writing and Editing Business Reports

Writing and editing business reports involves creating clear, concise, and well-structured documents that present information, analyses, and recommendations to support decision-making within an organization. This is another job AI handles extraordinarily well. The AI can comb through tens of thousands of documents, comparing market statistics and trends, giving you the exact data you need to make a decision.

10 potential prompt threads:

1. Define the purpose and audience of the report.
2. Gather and analyze relevant data and information.
3. Organize the report into sections, such as an introduction, analysis, and conclusion.
4. Write clear and concise content.
5. Use visual aids, such as charts and graphs, to illustrate data.
6. Use AI to generate report content based on input data.
7. Edit and proofread the report for clarity and accuracy.
8. Format the report professionally and consistently.
9. Summarize the report's key findings and recommendations.
10. Review and revise the report based on feedback.

When using AI for writing and editing business reports, ensure that the AI-generated content is accurate, clear, and logically structured. Always review and edit AI-generated content before publishing.

Further Resources:

1. Harvard Business Review (hbr.org): Offers articles and insights on various business topics, including communication and report writing.
2. Purdue OWL (owl.purdue.edu): Provides writing resources and instructional material on various writing styles, including business writing.
3. Grammarly Blog (grammarly.com/blog): Offers tips and guidelines on writing, grammar, punctuation, and style, which are useful for crafting well-written business reports.
4. "HBR Guide to Better Business Writing" by Bryan A. Garner (https://amzn.to/3A0hEL) - Offers practical tips and examples to help improve your business writing skills.
5. "The Business Writer's Handbook" by Gerald J. Alred, Charles T. Brusaw, and Walter E. Oliu (https://amzn.to/40at8GZ) - A comprehensive guide to various forms of business communication, including report writing.
6. "Writing That Works: How to Communicate Effectively in Business" by Kenneth Roman and Joel Raphaelson (https://amzn.to/41vjn7q) - Offers practical advice for writing various types of business documents, including reports.

Use Case 28:

Content Optimization for SEO

SEO (Search Engine Optimization) involves improving website content to increase its visibility in search engine results. When someone searches for the service your company provides, you want to be at the top of Google's list. When you optimize for SEO, you end up driving more organic traffic to your website and boosting site performance.

If this sounds like a hugely technical process, it definitely can be. With AI assistance though, you can take care of it quickly and easily. Here are 10 ideas that will allow you to use AI for search engine optimization:

1. Perform keyword research to identify relevant terms and phrases.
2. Optimize title tags and meta descriptions.
3. Incorporate keywords naturally into content.
4. Use header tags for better content structure.
5. Improve readability and user experience.
6. Optimize images and multimedia elements.
7. Implement internal and external linking strategies.
8. Use AI to analyze and optimize content for SEO.
9. Monitor and analyze website performance metrics.
10. Regularly update and refresh content to maintain relevance.

When using AI for SEO optimization, ensure that the AI-generated content is accurate, engaging, and adheres to search engine guidelines. Avoid keyword stuffing and focus on providing valuable content to users. The quality of the keywords, along with the content on your website, is more important than the quantity. If your blog articles are seen as being informative and helpful, Google and other search engines will be more likely to pass them along to potential customers.

Further Resources:

1. https://ahrefs.com/   Ahrefs is an SEO software suite that contains tools for link building, keyword research, competitor analysis, rank tracking and site audits. It is a popular choice among SEO professionals and marketers.
2. https://moz.com/ Moz is a marketing software company that provides SEO tools, competitive analysis, and other marketing solutions. It is also a popular choice among SEO professionals and marketers.

Use Case 29:

Writing Business Proposals and RFP Responses

Writing business proposals and RFP (Request for Proposal) responses involves crafting persuasive documents that showcase a company's capabilities, expertise, and proposed solutions. If you have good RFPs you can win more contracts or secure new business opportunities.

Using AI as a tool in this regard, companies can scan data it would take weeks to compile, while creating the proposals that will fit within your stated budgets. It can even compare what other businesses are offering with your own bids, making you more competitive.

10 potential prompt threads:

1. Thoroughly analyze the RFP or client requirements.
2. Define the project scope, objectives, and deliverables.
3. Develop a compelling value proposition.
4. Outline the proposed solution, methodology, and timeline.
5. Showcase your company's expertise, experience, and relevant case studies.
6. Provide a detailed budget and pricing structure.
7. Use AI to generate proposal content based on input data.
8. Edit and proofread the proposal for clarity and accuracy.

9. Format the proposal professionally and consistently.
10. Follow up with the client after submission.

When using AI for writing business proposals and RFP responses, ensure that the AI-generated content is accurate, persuasive, and tailored to the client's needs. Always review and edit AI-generated content before submitting.

Further Resources:

1. Association of Proposal Management Professionals (APMP) (apmp.org): Offers resources, best practices, and networking opportunities for proposal management professionals.
2. ProposalHelper (proposalhelper.com): Provides proposal writing resources, including tips, webinars, and blog posts, covering various aspects of the proposal process.
3. CapturePlanning.com (captureplanning.com): Offers articles, guides, and templates for writing and managing proposals.
4. "Writing Winning Business Proposals" by Richard C. Freed, Shervin Freed, and Joe Romano (https://amzn.to/3H7VGKH) - Offers practical advice and a step-by-step process for crafting successful business proposals.
5. "Proposal Development Secrets: Win More, Work Smarter, and Get Home on Time" by Matt Handal (https://amzn.to/43w8CU6) - Provides insights and strategies for writing compelling proposals that win more work.
6. "The One-Page Proposal: How to Get Your Business Pitch onto One Persuasive Page" by Patrick G. Riley (https://amzn.to/3A1WFrQ) - Presents a method for creating concise and compelling proposals that stand out to decision-makers.

Use Case 30:

Summarizing Lengthy Documents

Very few business owners have the time to read through extensive reports and market analyses. Most of the time all we want is a summary so we can make as informed a decision as possible. AI will do exactly that, shortening lengthy documents and condensing large volumes of text into shorter, more accessible summaries that capture the main ideas, findings, or conclusions while maintaining accuracy and coherence.

10 potential prompt threads:

1. Identify the main points and supporting evidence.
2. Eliminate unnecessary details and redundancies.
3. Use clear, concise language to convey the main ideas.
4. Maintain a neutral tone and avoid personal opinions or biases.
5. Format the summary for easy reading and comprehension.
6. Use AI to generate summaries based on input text.
7. Edit and proofread the summary for clarity and accuracy.
8. Ensure that the summary remains faithful to the original document.
9. Use summaries to support decision-making or information dissemination.

10. Implement AI-powered summarization tools within your organization.

Before putting all our trust in AI though, it's good to have someone familiar with the material being condensed verify the summary accurately represents the original content and maintains coherence. Always review and edit AI-generated summaries. Remember, the more details you give the AI, the better the results. If the prompts for the review were unclear, the summary could be heavily affected.

Further Resources:

1. https://www.smmry.com/ SMMRY is a website that provides summaries of articles, text, websites, essays, and documents.
2. https://www.autosummarizer.com/ AutoSummarizer is a website that provides automatic summaries of text.
3. https://www.goodreads.com Goodreads is a website that allows users to read and review books.

Use Case 31:

Data Visualization and Reporting

Generating insights from data, creating report templates, suggesting visualizations, or developing data-driven narratives is about the driest and most time-consuming task imaginable. The great thing about AI is that it can help make data more accessible, understandable, and actionable for decision-making. Plus, the sheer volume of insights it can supply will allow your business to see things that you otherwise would have missed.

Data is more important than ever, so here are 10 prompts that will get your AI platform spitting out insights that very well may help your company evolve:

1. Analyze a dataset and suggest key insights or trends.
2. Develop a report template for a specific department or function.
3. Suggest appropriate data visualizations for different types of data.
4. Write a data-driven narrative or story based on provided data.
5. Suggest strategies for improving data literacy within the organization.
6. Develop a list of key performance indicators (KPIs) for a specific department or function.
7. Create a dashboard layout for tracking business metrics.

8. Write a data analysis report for a specific project or initiative.
9. Develop a list of best practices for data visualization and reporting.
10. Suggest strategies for making data more accessible and actionable for decision-making.

If the AI-generated reporting isn't relevant or effective for your business, make sure you have given enough details in your prompts. The better the information you give to ChatGPT, the stronger the resource becomes.

Further Resources:

1. "Storytelling with Data" by Cole Nussbaumer Knaflic (https://amzn.to/41wkCmu) - Book on effective data visualization techniques.
2. FlowingData (https://flowingdata.com/) - Offers resources, insights, and best practices on data visualization and reporting.
3. "The Big Book of Dashboards" by Steve Wexler, Jeffrey Shaffer, and Andy Cotgreave (https://amzn.to/3L0eWvP) - Book on designing effective business dashboards.
4. Tableau (https://www.tableau.com/) - Provides resources, insights, and best practices on data visualization and business intelligence.

Use Case 32:

Creating Engaging Presentations

We've all attended conferences where the presenter gave a boring lecture, and everyone tuned out.

You don't want to make that mistake! Lucky for you (and all of us), AI can craft incredibly interesting presentations using innovative ideas that are on the forefront of business performance.

Creating engaging presentations involves designing visually appealing and informative slides that effectively convey information and ideas. The point of all of this is to capture and maintain the audience's attention.

10 potential prompt threads:

1. Define the purpose and audience for the presentation.
2. Organize content into a logical and coherent structure.
3. Use clear, concise language to convey key points.
4. Incorporate visual aids, such as images, charts, and graphs.
5. Use AI-powered tools to generate presentation content or design suggestions.
6. Ensure a consistent and professional visual design.
7. Practice and refine delivery and timing.
8. Encourage audience interaction and engagement.
9. Gather feedback on presentation effectiveness.
10. Continuously improve presentation skills and techniques.

When using AI for creating engaging presentations, ensure that the AI-generated content and design suggestions are relevant, accurate, and consistent with your brand guidelines. Always review and approve AI-generated changes before finalizing presentations.

Further Resources:

1. TED Talks (ted.com): Offers inspiring talks by expert speakers, showcasing engaging presentation styles and techniques.
2. SlideShare (slideshare.net): Provides a platform for sharing presentations and discovering new ideas, designs, and strategies for creating engaging slides.
3. Duarte (duarte.com): Offers blog posts, webinars, and resources on presentation design, storytelling, and public speaking; including "slide:ology: The Art and Science of Creating Great Presentations" by Nancy Duarte (https://amzn.to/3MKvppo)
4. "Presentation Zen: Simple Ideas on Presentation Design and Delivery" by Garr Reynolds (https://amzn.to/41r8S4Q) - Offers a guide to creating presentations that combine simplicity, clarity, and impact.
5. "Talk Like TED: The 9 Public-Speaking Secrets of the World's Top Minds" by Carmine Gallo(https://amzn.to/3GJLrf3) - Analyzes successful TED Talks and provides practical tips for creating and delivering engaging presentations.
6. "Resonate: Present Visual Stories that Transform Audiences" by Nancy Duarte (https://amzn.to/3Uz3wm1) - Offers a guide to creating compelling presentations that connect with the audience and inspire action.

Use Case 33:

Drafting External Communications

Drafting external communications involves creating written content for various channels and purposes, such as emails, newsletters, press releases, and social media posts, aimed at informing, engaging, or persuading target audiences.

When broken down, this is a massive amount of content depending on the size of your business. AI can create all of this content quickly, only needing an AI Whisperer to add good prompts and edit the communications before sending them out.

10 potential prompt threads:

1. Define the purpose, audience, and objectives of the communication.
2. Write clear, concise, and engaging content.
3. Ensure consistency with the company's style guide and brand voice.
4. Use appropriate tone and language for the target audience and channel.
5. Incorporate multimedia elements, such as images or videos, to enhance the message.
6. Use AI-powered tools to generate or optimize communication content.
7. Edit and proofread communications for clarity and accuracy.

8. Monitor and analyze the performance of communications.
9. Gather feedback from recipients and stakeholders.
10. Continuously improve communication strategies and techniques.

As always, when using AI for drafting external communications, you need to make sure the resulting content matches your company goals. Sometimes details can be wrong or misinterpreted, just like with a real person, so always have someone go through and edit the communications before you disseminate them to the public.

Further Resources:

Websites:

1. Ragan Communications (ragan.com): Offers articles, webinars, and resources on various aspects of corporate communications, including external communication best practices.
2. PR Daily (prdaily.com): Provides news, insights, and tips on public relations, media relations, and external communication strategies.
3. Business Writing Blog (businesswriting.com/blog): Offers practical advice and tips for writing clear, concise, and persuasive business communications, including external messages.
4. "Everybody Writes: Your Go-To Guide to Creating Ridiculously Good Content" by Ann Handley (https://amzn.to/3MILL1q) - Provides advice and insights for crafting compelling and effective external communications, including emails, social media posts, and blog articles.
5. "Made to Stick: Why Some Ideas Survive and Others Die" by Chip Heath and Dan Heath (https://amzn.to/3A2BRAp) - Offers

principles and techniques for creating memorable and engaging messages that resonate with your audience.

6. "The New Rules of Marketing and PR: How to Use Social Media, Online Video, Mobile Applications, Blogs, News Releases, and Viral Marketing to Reach Buyers Directly" by David Meerman Scott (https://amzn.to/3GIsidD) - Presents strategies for creating external communications that effectively reach and engage your target audience.

7. "The Art of Explanation: Making your Ideas, Products, and Services Easier to Understand" by Lee LeFever (https://amzn.to/3L1uU96) - Provides guidance on how to create clear, concise, and compelling explanations for complex topics in external communications.

8. "Writing Without Bullshit: Boost Your Career by Saying What You Mean" by Josh Bernoff (https://amzn.to/3mHO4at) - Offers practical tips for eliminating jargon, fluff, and unnecessary information in external communications, making them more concise and impactful.

9. Mailchimp (mailchimp.com): A marketing automation platform and email marketing service that helps businesses create, send, and analyze email campaigns.

10. Buffer (buffer.com): A social media management tool that allows businesses to schedule, publish, and analyze social media posts across multiple platforms.

Use Case 34:

Personalizing Customer Interactions

No customer wants to feel like they're so unimportant that a robot is the best they can expect to help them with their problems. A good AI though makes that problem mute. Most of the time the customer won't even know they're interacting with an artificial intelligence.

Personalizing customer interactions involves tailoring communication, content, and experiences based on individual customer preferences, behavior, and history to enhance engagement, satisfaction, and loyalty.

10 potential prompt threads:

1. Collect and analyze customer data to understand preferences and behavior.
2. Segment customers based on shared characteristics.
3. Customize content, offers, and recommendations for each segment.
4. Use AI-powered tools to automate personalization across channels.
5. Monitor and analyze the effectiveness of personalized interactions.
6. Continuously update customer profiles and preferences.

7. Ensure compliance with data privacy regulations and best practices.
8. Incorporate personalization into customer support and service interactions.
9. Test and optimize personalized communication strategies.
10. Use AI-generated insights to identify opportunities for further personalization.

When using AI for personalizing customer interactions, ensure that the AI-generated content and recommendations are relevant, accurate, and respectful of customer privacy. Remember, an AI doesn't actually think for itself. It's a tool that doesn't have the same discerning understanding a human has. Always make sure the details and final output are appropriate for your customers and business.

Further Resources:

1. HubSpot (hubspot.com): Offers resources, blog posts, and guides on customer relationship management, marketing, and personalization strategies.
2. ConstantContact (constantcontact.com),
3. Salesforce (salesforce.com): Provides resources and insights on customer engagement, personalization, and CRM best practices.
4. MarketingProfs (marketingprofs.com): Offers articles, webinars, and resources on various marketing topics, including customer personalization and engagement.
5. "Hug Your Haters: How to Embrace Complaints and Keep Your Customers" by Jay Baer(https://amzn.to/3L10WSw) Provides insights and strategies for handling customer interactions and personalizing your responses to create positive experiences.
6. "The Effortless Experience: Conquering the New Battleground for Customer Loyalty" by Matthew Dixon, Nick Toman, and Rick DeLisi (https://amzn.to/3UJQQsr) - Offers techniques for

improving customer interactions and personalizing service to increase satisfaction and loyalty.

7. "The Power of Moments: Why Certain Experiences Have Extraordinary Impact" by Chip Heath and Dan Heath (https://amzn.to/3zZrFIR) - Explores the importance of creating memorable and personalized experiences for customers and provides guidance on how to do so.

8. "Delivering Happiness: A Path to Profits, Passion, and Purpose" by Tony Hsieh (https://amzn.to/3mt1K9v) - Chronicles the success of Zappos and its focus on creating personalized and exceptional customer experiences.

9. https://www.optimizely.com/ Optimizely is a website that provides A/B testing, personalization, and optimization software.

10. https://www.segment.com/ Segment is a website that provides customer data infrastructure.

Use Case 35:

Process Improvement and Optimization

Employ ChatGPT to support your process improvement and optimization efforts by generating process maps, identifying inefficiencies, suggesting improvements, or creating standard operating procedures (SOPs). AI can help streamline operations, reduce costs, and enhance overall business performance.

Below are 10 different prompts that will yield promising results with AI assistance:

1. Create a process map for a specific operation or workflow.
2. Identify potential bottlenecks or inefficiencies in a given process.
3. Suggest improvements or optimizations for a particular process.
4. Write a standard operating procedure (SOP) for a specific task or function.
5. Develop a list of best practices for process improvement and optimization.
6. Create a performance measurement framework for evaluating process effectiveness.
7. Write a guide on implementing Lean or Six Sigma methodologies for process improvement.
8. Develop a list of potential process improvement tools or software solutions.

9. Suggest strategies for fostering a culture of continuous improvement within the organization.
10. Create a process improvement plan for a specific department or function.

When requesting process improvement and optimization assistance, provide specific information about your process, goals, and desired outcomes. If the AI-generated content is not relevant or effective, consider refining your prompt or providing additional context to better align with your process improvement goals.

Further Resources:

1. "The Goal" by Eliyahu M. Goldratt (https://amzn.to/41817DO) Book on process improvement and the Theory of Constraints.
2. Process Excellence Network (https://www.processexcellencenetwork.com/) - Offers resources, insights, and best practices on process improvement and optimization.
3. "Lean Thinking" by James P. Womack and Daniel T. Jones (https://amzn.to/3KvAGhu) - Book on Lean methodology and principles.
4. iSixSigma (https://www.isixsigma.com/) - Provides resources, insights, and best practices on Six Sigma and process improvement methodologies.

Use Case 36:

Writing Case Studies and Success Stories

Writing case studies and success stories involves creating detailed narratives that showcase the positive impact of your products, services, or solutions on customers. When done right, you provide evidence of value and build credibility with potential clients.

Once again, using an AI for this purpose will free up time for other pressing matters, while giving you a wealth of information to share internally or with the community at large.

10 potential prompt threads:

1. Identify customers with compelling success stories.
2. Gather relevant data, testimonials, and other supporting evidence.
3. Structure the narrative to include background, challenges, solutions, and results.
4. Use clear, concise language to convey the story.
5. Incorporate visuals, such as images or charts, to enhance the presentation.
6. Use AI-powered tools to generate case study content based on input data.
7. Edit and proofread case studies for clarity and accuracy.
8. Promote case studies on your website, social media, and other marketing channels.

9. Monitor the performance and impact of case studies on lead generation and sales.
10. Continuously update and expand your library of case studies and success stories.

Writing case studies and success stories gives you another avenue to present content to either your customers or shareholders. To ensure that the AI-generated content is accurate, engaging, and consistent with your organization's style guide and brand voice, make sure to have a trusted manager go over every piece of content. You don't want to get your company in trouble by simply taking what the AI gives you and putting it out into the world.

Further Resources:

1. HubSpot (hubspot.com): Offers resources, templates, and blog posts on creating compelling case studies and success stories for marketing purposes.
2. Content Marketing Institute (contentmarketinginstitute.com): Provides articles, guides, and resources on various content marketing topics, including case study and success story creation.
3. "The Case Study Handbook: How to Read, Discuss, and Write Persuasively About Cases" by William Ellet (https://amzn.to/3L0t2gN) - Offers guidance on analyzing, discussing, and writing about business case studies, with a focus on persuasive storytelling.
4. "Case Study Research: Design and Methods" by Robert K. Yin (https://amzn.to/3mFqviv) - Provides a comprehensive guide to conducting case study research and presenting the findings effectively.
5. "Stories That Sell: Turn Satisfied Customers into Your Most Powerful Sales & Marketing Asset" by Casey Hibbard (https://amzn.to/3KGzmZz) - Offers strategies and techniques for

creating compelling success stories and case studies that showcase the value of your products or services.

Use Case 37:

Managing Content Calendars and Editorial Plans

Organization is a key component in managing content calendars and editorial plans. Luckily, AI is about as organized as you can get. Sometimes ChatGPT will throw you a curveball that makes you chuckle, but for the most part, AI has their ducks in a row. Scheduling the creation, publication, and promotion of content across various channels and formats is one of artificial intelligence's strengths. It will support marketing, communication, and business objectives.

10 potential prompt threads:

1. Define content goals, objectives, and target audiences.
2. Identify relevant content topics and formats.
3. Develop a content calendar that outlines publication dates and channels.
4. Use AI-powered tools to generate content ideas and optimize publishing schedules.
5. Assign content creation tasks to team members or external contributors.
6. Monitor and analyze the performance of published content.
7. Adjust content plans based on performance data and audience feedback.
8. Ensure content is aligned with broader marketing and communication strategies.

9. Regularly update and refine content plans to stay relevant and engaging.
10. Use AI-generated insights to identify opportunities for content optimization.

When using AI for managing content calendars and editorial plans, ensure that the ideas and recommendations support your company goals, objectives, and brand voice. Always review and approve AI-generated suggestions before incorporating them into your content plans.

Further Resources:

1. Trello (Trello.com) excels in providing a visually appealing and intuitive platform for managing tasks and projects using the Kanban methodology, making it easy for teams to collaborate and track progress.
2. Airtable (airtable.com) shines in its ability to handle complex data through a flexible, customizable database, offering multiple views and powerful features for organizing and analyzing information.
3. Asana (asana.com): A project management platform that can be used to create content calendars, assign tasks, set deadlines, and collaborate on editorial plans.
4. CoSchedule (coschedule.com): A content marketing platform specifically designed for planning, organizing, and executing content marketing and social media campaigns.
5. Google Calendar (calendar.google.com): A widely used calendar tool that can be adapted for managing content calendars and editorial plans by creating events, setting reminders, and sharing calendars with team members.
6. Monday.com (monday.com): A work operating system that allows you to create customizable boards for managing content calendars, tracking tasks, and collaborating on editorial plans.

7. ContentCal (contentcal.io): A content marketing and social media planning platform that helps you plan, create, and publish content while collaborating with your team.

8. "Work Smarter Not Harder: 18 Productivity Tips That Boost Your Work Day Performance" by Timo Kiander (https://amzn.to/411axyh) - Offers productivity tips and strategies that can be applied to various aspects of work, including content management and automation.

9. "Automate This: How Algorithms Came to Rule Our World" by Christopher Steiner (https://amzn.to/3UCDMVK) - Explores the power of automation and algorithms in various industries and provides insights that can be applied to content calendar management and editorial planning.

10. "The One-Minute To-Do List: Quickly Get Your Chaos Completely Under Control" by Michael Linenberger (https://amzn.to/3UzXx0f) - Offers time management and productivity techniques that can help you better manage and automate your content calendars and editorial plans.

Use Case 38:

Developing Creative Advertising Concepts

Marketing can be a beast. Let's be honest. We know we have to spend money to advertise, but often it's like throwing darts at a board to determine what works and what doesn't.

Data is the saving grace in advertising, and no one has more data than AI. They have access to the width and breadth of human knowledge and can see things even trained marketers miss.

AI can develop creative advertising concepts and generate unique, engaging ideas for marketing campaigns that effectively communicate brand messages, capture audience attention, and drive desired actions.

Here are 10 ideas that will allow you to use AI to maximum efficiency:

1. Define the advertising campaign's goals, objectives, and target audience.
2. Research industry trends, competitor campaigns, and audience preferences.
3. Generate creative ideas through brainstorming, mind mapping, or other ideation techniques.
4. Use AI-powered tools to generate advertising concepts based on input data.
5. Develop a unique selling proposition (USP) that differentiates your brand or product.

6. Create compelling visuals, copy, and messaging that support the advertising concept.
7. Test and refine advertising concepts based on audience feedback and performance data.
8. Ensure advertising concepts align with your overall brand strategy and guidelines.
9. Execute and monitor the advertising campaign across various channels.
10. Continuously improve advertising concepts and strategies based on performance metrics and industry trends.

Always review and refine AI-generated concepts before incorporating them into your advertising campaigns. There are a lot of nuances when it comes to marketing. Use these artificial intelligence ideas as a base for what comes next. AI doesn't replace your marketing team; it just gives them a leg-up on the competition.

Further Resources:

1. Adweek (adweek.com): Offers news, insights, and resources on advertising, media, and marketing, including articles on creative advertising concepts and trends.
2. AdAge (adage.com): Provides news, analysis, and insights on advertising, marketing, and media, featuring articles on creative advertising concepts, case studies, and campaigns.
3. The Drum (thedrum.com): Covers news and opinions on marketing, advertising, and design, with articles on creative advertising concepts, trends, and best practices.
4. Creative Bloq (creativebloq.com): Offers articles, resources, and inspiration on graphic design, branding, and advertising, including tips and ideas for developing creative advertising concepts.
5. Ads of the World (adsoftheworld.com): Showcases creative advertising campaigns from around the world, providing

inspiration and insights into developing innovative advertising concepts.

6. "Hey, Whipple, Squeeze This: The Classic Guide to Creating Great Ads" by Luke Sullivan (https://amzn.to/3GKBfTK) - Offers practical advice and insights for creating compelling and effective advertising concepts.

7. "Ogilvy on Advertising" by David Ogilvy (https://amzn.to/3A0K4Fi) - Provides timeless insights and advice on advertising from one of the industry's most respected figures.

8. "The Idea Writers: Copywriting in a New Media and Marketing Era" by Teressa Iezzi (https://amzn.to/3ojKnIo) Offers guidance on crafting compelling advertising concepts in the digital age, with insights from leading creative professionals.

9. "Truth, Lies, and Advertising: The Art of Account Planning" by Jon Steel (https://amzn.to/418VUZX) - Presents techniques for developing advertising strategies and creative concepts based on consumer insights and research.

10. "The Copy Book: How 32 of the World's Best Advertising Writers Write Their Advertising" by D&AD (https://amzn.to/411bPJD) - Showcases advertising concepts and copywriting techniques from top industry professionals, providing inspiration and ideas for developing your own creative advertising concepts.

Use Case 39:

Sales Strategy and Pipeline Management

Utilize ChatGPT to support your sales strategy and pipeline management efforts by generating sales scripts, email templates, lead qualification criteria, or sales performance metrics. AI can help improve sales processes, boost conversion rates, and enhance overall revenue generation.

10 Potential Prompt Threads:

1. Write a sales script for a specific product or service offering.
2. Develop a sales email template for prospecting or follow-up.
3. Create a list of lead qualification criteria for a particular target market.
4. Suggest strategies for improving sales pipeline management and conversion rates.
5. Write a guide on best practices for conducting effective sales calls or meetings.
6. Develop a list of potential sales performance metrics or KPIs.
7. Create a sales strategy for penetrating a new market or customer segment.
8. Write a guide on using specific sales tools or software (e.g., CRM systems).

9. Develop a list of potential sales training resources or materials.
10. Suggest strategies for handling sales objections or negotiating deals.

When requesting sales strategy and pipeline management assistance, provide specific information about your product, target market, or sales process. If the AI-generated content is not relevant or effective, consider refining your prompt or providing additional context to better align with your sales goals.

Further Resources:

1. HubSpot (hubspot.com): Offers resources, blog posts, and guides on sales strategy, pipeline management, and customer relationship management.
2. Sales Hacker (saleshacker.com): Provides articles, webinars, and resources on various sales topics, including sales strategy, pipeline management, and sales enablement.
3. Salesforce (salesforce.com): Offers insights, resources, and blog posts on sales strategy, pipeline management, and CRM best practices.
4. Sandler Training (sandler.com): Provides sales training resources, articles, and podcasts on sales strategy, pipeline management, and sales techniques.
5. CloserIQ (closeriq.com): Offers blog posts, articles, and resources on sales strategy, pipeline management, and sales team development.
6. "The Challenger Sale" by Matthew Dixon and Brent Adamson (https://amzn.to/3MKyxl4) - Book on a new approach to sales and customer engagement
7. "SPIN Selling" by Neil Rackham (https://amzn.to/3GJClzg) - Book on consultative selling and sales techniques.

8. "New Sales. Simplified.: The Essential Handbook for Prospecting and New Business Development" by Mike Weinberg (https://amzn.to/41wvqky) Offers practical advice and strategies for developing a successful sales strategy and managing your sales pipeline.

9. "Cracking the Sales Management Code: The Secrets to Measuring and Managing Sales Performance" by Jason Jordan and Michelle Vazzana (https://amzn.to/3L02GeF) - Provides insights and techniques for managing sales performance and sales pipelines effectively.

10. "The Sales Acceleration Formula: Using Data, Technology, and Inbound Selling to Go from $0 to $100 Million" by Mark Roberge (https://amzn.to/3og7HXJ) - Offers guidance on building a scalable and predictable sales strategy using data, technology, and inbound selling.

11. "Predictable Revenue: Turn Your Business into a Sales Machine with the $100 Million Best Practices of Salesforce.com" by Aaron Ross and Marylou Tyler (https://amzn.to/3AiNfs9) - Provides insights into the strategies and techniques used by Salesforce.com to create a scalable and predictable sales process, including prospecting, lead generation, and pipeline management; and it's one of those books when I read it set my mind on fire with creativity. I highly recommend it.

Use Case 40:

Brainstorming Ideas and Solutions

A good idea is worth a million dollars…sometimes a billion. We've all sat in brainstorming sessions spit-balling ideas long into the night. The great thing about AI is that it can give us tons of ideas at the click of a button, so long as we know what questions to ask. Use ChatGPT to brainstorm ideas and solutions for various challenges and opportunities within your business. AI can help generate creative, out-of-the-box ideas, assist in problem-solving, and offer fresh perspectives to fuel innovation and growth.

10 Potential Prompt Threads:

1. Generate five ideas for increasing our customer retention rate.
2. Suggest three potential solutions to streamline our internal communication process.
3. Brainstorm new features or improvements for our existing product line.
4. Come up with five strategies to boost our social media engagement.
5. Help me identify potential areas for cost reduction within our operations.
6. Suggest three initiatives to improve our company culture and employee satisfaction.

7. Propose ideas for expanding our services to new markets or industries.
8. Brainstorm potential partnerships or collaborations that could benefit our business.
9. Offer three ideas for improving our website's user experience.
10. Generate five marketing campaign concepts to drive brand awareness.

When requesting brainstorming assistance, provide sufficient context and specify the desired outcome. The AI can only work with the information you give it. Always be ready to clarify or ask more questions, particularly when looking for good ideas. And like with a normal brainstorming session, some of the ideas are going to be duds; you'll just be able to get through those duds faster so you can find the diamonds in the rough.

Further Resources:

1. "Types of Innovation" by Larry Keely (https://amzn.to/3L2M32f) - Relates ten scopes of innovation around a wheel with ideation exercises. Also known as the Doblin method.
2. "Doblin Innovation Tactics Cards," by Doblin (https://amzn.to/40aJGOQ) based on the Ten Types of Innovation Method. Wonderful for executives and teams to use as fire starters for new ideas, processes, and products.
3. MindTools (https://www.mindtools.com/cx4ems0/problem-solving) - Offers resources and tools for brainstorming and problem-solving.
4. "Thinkertoys" by Michael Michalko – (https://amzn.to/3ohdVGB) - Book on creative thinking techniques and strategies.

5. Ideo Blog (https://www.ideo.com/blog) - Shares insights and tips on innovation and design thinking.

6. "Creative Confidence" by Tom Kelley and David Kelley (https://amzn.to/3KYGd1K) - Book on nurturing creativity and innovation in organizations.

Use Case 41
ChatGPT as an MS Excel Workbook Terminal

AI can help users with Excel functions, formulas, and data analysis techniques to improve decision-making and enhance overall business performance. Creating a powerful spreadsheet solves numerous business problems, and when you have an AI that can create more than one at the same time, you find possibilities opening up right before your eyes. You can then solve complex business problems by emulating an MS Excel Workbook terminal.

If you need help with workbooks and Excel functions, we have 10 potential prompts for you right here:

1. Write a step-by-step guide on performing a specific Excel function or operation.
2. Suggest formulas or techniques for analyzing a particular dataset.
3. Develop a list of best practices for data management in Excel.
4. Provide guidance on using Excel for financial modeling or forecasting.
5. Write a tutorial on creating charts or visualizations in Excel.
6. Develop a list of Excel keyboard shortcuts or tips for increased productivity.
7. Create a guide on using Excel add-ins or third-party tools to enhance functionality.

8. Write a step-by-step guide on creating a custom macro in Excel.
9. Develop a list of common Excel errors and their solutions.
10. Suggest strategies for optimizing Excel performance and reducing file sizes.

When requesting assistance with Excel, provide specific information about your desired function, operation, or data analysis goal. The employee acting as your AI Whisperer in this case needs to have a good understanding of Excel and the math involved in creating the proper functions. If they do, you'll be able to create all sorts of workbooks to help your company succeed.

Further Resources:

1. Excel 2023: Up to date guide to master all the MS Excel Fundamentals,' by Fletcher Dinkins (https://amzn.to/3A58Js0).
2. Exceljet (https://exceljet.net/) - Offers resources, insights, and best practices on Microsoft Excel.
3. MrExcel (https://www.mrexcel.com/) - Provides resources, insights, and best practices on Excel usage and techniques.
4. 80 Useful Excel Chat GPT Prompts to 10x Your Excel Skills (https://www.greataiprompts.com/chat-gpt/excel-chat-gpt-prompts/)

Use Case 42:

ChatGPT as a JavaScript Console

Leverage ChatGPT to assist with solving complex business problems by emulating a JavaScript console. AI can help users with JavaScript functions, debugging, and coding techniques to improve web development and enhance overall website performance.

Again, the AI doesn't replace your web team, it merely gives them tools to speed up processes and verify common mistakes are avoided.

10 Potential Prompt Threads:

1. Write a step-by-step guide on performing a specific JavaScript function or operation.
2. Suggest JavaScript code snippets or solutions for a particular problem.
3. Develop a list of best practices for JavaScript coding and optimization.
4. Provide guidance on using JavaScript for web development or interactivity.
5. Write a tutorial on implementing common JavaScript libraries or frameworks.
6. Develop a list of JavaScript debugging techniques or tools.

7. Create a guide on using browser developer tools for JavaScript console operations.
8. Write a step-by-step guide on implementing a custom JavaScript event listener.
9. Develop a list of common JavaScript errors and their solutions.
10. Suggest strategies for optimizing JavaScript performance and reducing page load times.

Always provide specific information about your desired function, operation, or coding goal when using AI with JavaScript. Just like in any coding scenario, small mistakes in the code will perpetuate big problems, so your AI Whisperer will need to pay attention to every prompt they use with the artificial intelligence. If the AI-generated content is not relevant or effective, consider refining your prompt or providing additional context to better align with your JavaScript-related needs.

Further Resources:

1. Visual Studio Code (code.visualstudio.com): A popular code editor with built-in support for JavaScript and extensions for various programming languages and frameworks.
2. Node.js (nodejs.org): A JavaScript runtime environment that allows you to execute JavaScript code on the server-side, which can be useful when interacting with APIs like ChatGPT.
3. Mozilla Developer Network (MDN) (developer.mozilla.org): Offers comprehensive documentation, guides, and tutorials on JavaScript, including best practices and examples.
4. W3Schools (w3schools.com): Provides tutorials, examples, and reference materials on JavaScript, HTML, CSS, and other web development technologies.

5. JavaScript.info (javascript.info): Offers in-depth tutorials and guides on JavaScript, covering various aspects of the language and its usage.

6. Stack Overflow (stackoverflow.com): A popular Q&A platform for developers, where you can find answers to JavaScript-related questions and issues.

7. "Eloquent JavaScript: A Modern Introduction to Programming" by Marijn Haverbeke: Provides a comprehensive introduction to JavaScript and programming concepts, with practical examples and exercises.

8. "You Don't Know JS" (book series) by Kyle Simpson: A series of books that cover various aspects of JavaScript in-depth, helping you gain a deep understanding of the language.

9. "JavaScript: The Good Parts" by Douglas Crockford: Offers insights into the best practices and powerful features of JavaScript, helping you write effective and efficient code.

10. Mozilla Developer Network (https://developer.mozilla.org/) - Offers resources, insights, and best practices on JavaScript and web development.

11. "JavaScript: The Definitive Guide" by David Flanagan - Comprehensive book on JavaScript programming.

.

Use Case 43:

ChatGPT as a Python Script Coder

As long as we're talking about coding, you can also employ ChatGPT to assist with solving complex business problems by emulating a Python script coder. AI can help users with Python functions, libraries, and coding techniques to improve software development and enhance overall project performance.

Here are 10 potential prompt threads to get you going with AI as a Python script coder:

1. Write a step-by-step guide on performing a specific Python function or operation.
2. Suggest Python code snippets or solutions for a particular problem.
3. Develop a list of best practices for Python coding and optimization.
4. Provide guidance on using Python for data analysis, web development, or automation.
5. Write a tutorial on implementing common Python libraries or frameworks.
6. Develop a list of Python debugging techniques or tools.
7. Create a guide on setting up a Python development environment.
8. Write a step-by-step guide on implementing a custom Python class or function.

9. Develop a list of common Python errors and their solutions.
10. Suggest strategies for optimizing Python performance and code readability.

When requesting assistance with Python, provide specific information about your desired function, operation, or coding goal. Having a coder go over everything is a 100% necessity. Redundancies are always necessary, whether you're working with a human coder or an AI. Everything needs to be checked and rechecked either way.

Further Resources:

1. Visual Studio Code (code.visualstudio.com): A popular code editor with built-in support for Python and extensions for various programming languages and frameworks.
2. PyCharm (jetbrains.com/pycharm): A powerful and feature-rich integrated development environment (IDE) specifically designed for Python development.
3. Python.org (python.org): The official website for Python, offering comprehensive documentation, tutorials, and guides.
4. Real Python (realpython.com): Provides in-depth tutorials, articles, and resources on various Python topics, from beginner to advanced levels.
5. W3Schools (w3schools.com/python): Offers tutorials, examples, and reference materials on Python and related technologies.
6. Stack Overflow (stackoverflow.com): A popular Q&A platform for developers, where you can find answers to Python-related questions and issues.
7. "Python Crash Course" by Eric Matthes: A comprehensive introduction to Python programming, including practical projects and examples.

8. "Automate the Boring Stuff with Python" by Al Sweigart: Teaches Python programming through practical examples, focusing on automating everyday tasks.
9. "Fluent Python: Clear, Concise, and Effective Programming" by Luciano Ramalho: Offers insights into Python best practices, idiomatic expressions, and advanced features.
10. "Effective Python: 90 Specific Ways to Write Better Python" by Brett Slatkin: Provides practical tips and best practices for writing clean, efficient, and maintainable Python code.

Use Case 44:

AI as a Business Process API Connector

Utilize ChatGPT to assist with solving complex business problems by acting as a business process API connector for CRMs, ERPs, and other systems. AI can help users with API integration, development, and optimization to improve data flow, automation, and overall business efficiency.

10 Potential Prompt Threads:

1. Write a step-by-step guide on connecting a specific CRM or ERP system via API.
2. Suggest API integration solutions for data synchronization or automation.
3. Develop a list of best practices for API development and management.
4. Provide guidance on using API connectors for business process improvement.
5. Write a tutorial on implementing common API authentication methods.
6. Develop a list of API debugging techniques or tools.
7. Create a guide on setting up a development environment for API integration.
8. Write a step-by-step guide on implementing a custom API endpoint.
9. Develop a list of common API errors and their solutions.

10. Suggest strategies for optimizing API performance and security.

When requesting assistance with API integration, provide specific information about your desired system, operation, or integration goal. If the AI-generated content is not relevant or effective, consider refining your prompt or providing additional context to better align with your API-related needs.

Further Resources:

1. "RESTful API Design" by Matthias Biehl - Book on designing and implementing RESTful APIs.
2. ProgrammableWeb (https://www.programmableweb.com/) - Offers resources, insights, and best practices on API development and integration.
3. "APIs: A Strategy Guide" by Daniel Jacobson, Greg Brail, and Dan Woods - Book on API strategy and management.
4. Postman Blog (https://blog.postman.com/) - Provides resources, insights, and best practices on API development and testing.
5. Exploring the Capabilities of the ChatGPT API: A beginners guide, by Dilip Kashyap, https://levelup.gitconnected.com/exploring-the-capabilities-of-the-chatgpt-api-a-beginners-guide-e9089d49961f

Use Case 45:

ChatGPT for Legacy Machines and IoT Integration

Leverage artificial intelligence to assist with connecting legacy machines to the internet and integrating IoT solutions, providing resources, analysis, and process improvements. IoT solutions help build networks of IoT devices, reducing complication, ensuring device effectiveness, and driving innovation across industries looking for chances to grow. AI can help users with IoT development, data management, and system optimization to enhance overall business efficiency.

10 Potential Prompt Threads:

1. Write a step-by-step guide on connecting a specific legacy machine to the internet.
2. Suggest IoT integration solutions for data collection and automation.
3. Develop a list of best practices for IoT development and management.
4. Provide guidance on using IoT solutions for business process improvement.
5. Write a tutorial on implementing common IoT communication protocols.
6. Develop a list of IoT debugging techniques or tools.

7. Create a guide on setting up a development environment for IoT integration.
8. Write a step-by-step guide on implementing a custom IoT sensor or device.
9. Develop a list of common IoT errors and their solutions.
10. Suggest strategies for optimizing IoT performance and security.

If you're using AI with IoT integration or legacy machine connectivity, provide specific information about your desired system, operation, or integration ambitions. If the AI-generated content is not relevant or operational, reword your prompts or provide additional context to better support your IoT-related needs.

Further Resources:

1. "Internet of Things for Architects" by Perry Lea - Book on IoT architecture and integration.
2. IoT World Today (https://www.iotworldtoday.com/) - Offers resources, insights, and best practices on IoT development and management.
3. "Building the Internet of Things" by Maciej Kranz - Book on IoT strategy and implementation.
4. IoT For All (https://www.iotforall.com/) - Provides resources, insights, and best practices on IoT development, use cases, and trends.
5. "Introducing ChatGPT and Whisper APIs," by OpenAI.com, https://openai.com/blog/introducing-chatgpt-and-whisper-apis

Use Case 46:

Solving Employee Engagement Problems

People are always the X-Factor in business. Sometimes teams don't get along, and finding reasons can be difficult.

AI can help with that, merely for the fact that it can process so much data and give you ideas on what the problems could be, along with solutions that have worked at other companies.

Let's look at this problem a bit differently and give you another way to think about your prompts and how to use AI as a business tool using the 'Five Why's' Strategy that executive coaches may use to learn more about engagement or the lack thereof.

Level 1: Identify the problem.

Prompt: Help me identify common employee engagement problems and potential causes.

Level 2: Explore solutions.

Prompt: Provide a list of strategies to address the employee engagement problems identified in level 1.

Level 3: Develop a plan.

Prompt: Create a step-by-step plan to implement the strategies from level 2 to improve employee engagement.

Level 4: Monitor progress.

Prompt: Suggest methods for tracking the effectiveness of the employee engagement strategies and identifying areas for improvement.

Level 5: Adjust and optimize.

Prompt: Recommend ways to optimize the employee engagement plan based on the progress monitoring results from level.

The issue remains that employee engagement is challenging in the current hybrid work environment with some workers in the office full time, others hybrid, and others remote.

Here are 10 questions threads or prompts you might consider asking ChatGPT for assistance on employee engagement matters.

1. How can I identify the root causes of disengagement in my team?
2. What are some effective ways to improve employee engagement in a remote work environment?
3. How can I measure and track employee engagement in my organization?
4. What role do managers play in driving employee engagement and how can they improve their effectiveness?
5. What are some best practices for creating a positive work culture that promotes engagement and motivation?
6. How can I use technology to support employee engagement and communication in a remote work setting?
7. What are some effective strategies for recognizing and rewarding employee contributions and achievements?

8. How can I create opportunities for professional growth and development that increase employee engagement and retention?
9. What are some common mistakes to avoid when trying to improve employee engagement?
10. How can I effectively communicate with my team about changes in organizational goals and values that impact engagement?

Further Resources:

1. "The Employee Experience Advantage: How to Win the War for Talent by Giving Employees the Workspaces they Want, the Tools they Need, and a Culture They Can Celebrate" by Jacob Morgan (https://amzn.to/415zybA)
2. "The Engagement Equation: Leadership Strategies for an Inspired Workforce" by Christopher Rice, Fraser Marlow, and Mary Ann Masarech (https://amzn.to/3GJh0FU)
3. "Drive: The Surprising Truth About What Motivates Us" by Daniel H. Pink (https://amzn.to/41bglFB)
4. "The Power of Moments: Why Certain Experiences Have Extraordinary Impact" by Chip Heath and Dan Heath (https://amzn.to/3zZrFIR)
5. "Dare to Lead: Brave Work. Tough Conversations. Whole Hearts." by Brené Brown (https://amzn.to/3UEFKF9)
6. "tate of the Global Workplace: 2022 Report," Gallup's Employee Engagement Center: https://www.gallup.com/workplace/349484/state-of-the-global-workplace-2022-report.aspx
7. The Society for Human Resource Management (SHRM): https://www.shrm.org/
8. Harvard Business Review (HBR): https://hbr.org/
9. Bersin by Deloitte: https://www.bersin.com/
10. Employee Engagement Institute: https://www.employeeengagement.com/
11. TED Talks on Employee Engagement: https://www.ted.com/topics/employee+engagement
12. Employee Engagement Surveys: Survey Monkey, Qualtrics, and Culture Amp are popular survey tools that can help HR managers

measure employee engagement levels and gather feedback on how to improve it.

13. LinkedIn Learning: Offers a range of online courses on leadership, employee engagement, and team building that can be helpful for HR managers and business leaders.

Use Case 47:

Enhancing Brand Storytelling

Enhancing brand storytelling involves crafting compelling narratives that communicate your organization's values, purpose, and personality. With AI as a tool, you can create emotional connections with your audience and differentiate your brand from competitors. Honestly, it's incredibly fun feeding ChatGPT different prompts and allowing it to create narratives that support your brand. Sometimes what it comes with is crazy and unusable, but more often than not, you get content that really opens your eyes to the potential of AI.

10 potential prompt threads:

1. Define your brand's core values, mission, and unique selling proposition.
2. Identify key moments, achievements, or milestones in your organization's history.
3. Develop relatable and engaging brand stories that resonate with your target audience.
4. Use AI-powered tools to generate and optimize brand storytelling ideas and narratives.
5. Incorporate brand storytelling elements into various marketing materials and communications.
6. Use multimedia formats, such as videos, podcasts, or interactive content, to enhance brand storytelling.

7. Test and refine brand stories based on audience feedback and performance metrics.
8. Monitor and analyze the impact of brand storytelling on audience engagement and brand perception.
9. Collaborate with influencers, partners, or customers to amplify your brand stories.
10. Continuously improve brand storytelling strategies based on audience needs and industry trends.

When using AI for enhancing brand storytelling, ensure that the AI-generated ideas and narratives align with your organization's values, objectives, and brand guidelines. Always review and refine AI-generated stories before incorporating them into your marketing efforts to ensure they effectively communicate your desired message.

Further Resources:

1. "Building a StoryBrand: Clarify Your Message So Customers Will Listen" by Donald Miller (https://amzn.to/3UEtGUm)
2. "The Art of Storytelling: Easy Steps to Presenting an Unforgettable Story" by John D. Walsh (https://amzn.to/3KHLx8e)
3. "Made to Stick: Why Some Ideas Survive and Others Die" by Chip Heath and Dan Heath (https://amzn.to/3A2BRAp)
4. "Brand Storytelling: Put Customers at the Heart of Your Brand Story" by Miri Rodriguez (https://amzn.to/43xJdtb)
5. "Storynomics: Story-Driven Marketing in the Post-Advertising World" by Robert Mckee and Tom Gerace (https://amzn.to/3UCfpHD)
6. HubSpot: https://www.hubspot.com/
7. The Content Marketing Institute: https://contentmarketinginstitute.com/
8. MarketingProfs: https://www.marketingprofs.com/

9. AdWeek: https://www.adweek.com/
10. Branding Strategy Insider:
    https://www.brandingstrategyinsider.com/
11. TED Talks on Storytelling:
    https://www.ted.com/topics/storytelling
12. Canva: Canva is a design tool that can be used to create visually appealing and engaging brand materials.
13. Hootsuite: Hootsuite is a social media management tool that can help businesses effectively communicate their brand message and storytelling on various social media platforms.
14. LinkedIn Learning: Offers a range of online courses on brand building, storytelling, and content marketing that can be helpful for businesses and marketers.

Use Case 48:

Developing a Marketing Plan

We talked about writing marketing copy in our very first Use Case. AI is great for that. But don't let your advertising ideas stop there. It's actually possible to create entire marketing plans with the help of AI, if you know what prompts to use.

Below are 5 steps that will allow your team to take advantage of ChatGPT technology in formulating entire marketing strategies.

Level 1: Establish goals.

Prompt: Help me define SMART marketing goals for my business based on its current situation and objectives.

Level 2: Select strategies.

Prompt: Provide a list of marketing strategies that align with the goals established in level 1.

Level 3: Develop a plan.

Prompt: Create a detailed marketing plan, including a timeline and budget, based on the strategies identified in level 2.

Level 4: Monitor progress.

Prompt: Suggest key performance indicators (KPIs) and

methods for tracking the effectiveness of the marketing plan from level 3.

Level 5: Adjust and optimize.

Prompt: Recommend ways to refine and optimize the marketing plan based on the progress monitoring results from level 4. Repeat if necessary.

Like with so many other aspects of AI we've discussed over the course of this book, your advertising team is an integral part in this process. Artificial intelligence is one more tool to help them reach the highest of goals. As they learn to create dozens of potential ad campaigns, all it will do is open up even more options for their success.

10 prompts you might consider using with ChatGPT to go deeper on the marketing plan issue:

1. What are some effective strategies for identifying and targeting my ideal customer segments?
2. How can I create a compelling brand message that resonates with my target audience?
3. Given my industry, what are 5 marketing personas that I should pay attention to? In your response provide the revenue, behavior, concerns, and buying habits for each persona.
4. What are some best practices for creating engaging content that drives customer engagement and conversions?
5. How can I leverage social media to reach and engage with my target audience effectively?
6. What are some effective ways to measure and analyze the effectiveness of my marketing campaigns?
7. How can I stay up-to-date on the latest marketing trends and technologies to improve my marketing strategy?

8. How can I optimize my website and other digital assets to improve my search engine rankings and drive more traffic to my site?
9. What are some effective ways to integrate different marketing channels to create a cohesive and impactful marketing plan?
10. How can I leverage customer feedback and data to continually improve my marketing strategy and customer experience?

Resources

1. HubSpot: https://www.hubspot.com/marketing
2. MarketingProfs: https://www.marketingprofs.com/
3. The Content Marketing Institute: https://contentmarketinginstitute.com/
4. Moz: https://moz.com/
5. Social Media Examiner: https://www.socialmediaexaminer.com/
6. Books:
7. "Building a StoryBrand: Clarify Your Message So Customers Will Listen" by Donald Miller (https://amzn.to/3UEtGUm)
8. "Contagious: Why Things Catch On" by Jonah Berger (https://amzn.to/3GMIxqa)
9. "Epic Content Marketing: How to Tell a Different Story, Break through the Clutter, and Win More Customers by Marketing Less" by Joe Pulizzi (https://amzn.to/43xM99a)
10. "The 1-Page Marketing Plan: Get New Customers, Make More Money, And Stand Out From The Crowd" by Allan Dib (https://amzn.to/3zXccZV)
11. "Digital Marketing for Dummies" by Ryan Deiss and Russ Henneberry (https://amzn.to/3GK2ZYw)
12. Hootsuite Academy: https://education.hootsuite.com/
13. Google Analytics Academy: https://analytics.google.com/analytics/academy/
14. LinkedIn Learning: Offers a range of online courses on marketing, branding, and digital marketing that can be helpful for business users.
15. The American Marketing Association: https://www.ama.org/
16. The Small Business Administration (SBA): https://www.sba.gov/business-guide/marketing/marketing-plan

Use Case 49:

Launching a New Business

Much like advertising, starting a new business can be a crapshoot. You may have an idea that seems like the greatest thing since air conditioning, but often we're too close to the process of building a company to see whether our idea is actually any good. That is where AI comes in. Dispassionate and precise, artificial intelligence will go through terabytes of data and let us know whether we have the next Google on our hands, or a mouse trap that can't catch mice.

Here is one potential process for testing your new business idea:

Level 1: Define the concept.

Prompt: Help me create a clear and concise business concept statement based on my initial idea.

Level 2: Develop a business plan.

Prompt: Provide an outline for a comprehensive business plan, including key sections and content to cover.

Level 3: Identify resources.

Prompt: List the resources, such as funding, equipment, and personnel, required to launch the new business based on the plan from level 2.

Level 4: Create a launch plan.

Prompt: Develop a step-by-step launch plan, including a timeline and milestones, to bring the new business to market.

Level 5: Monitor and adjust.

Prompt: Suggest methods for tracking the success of the new business launch and identifying areas for improvement or adjustment.

Given that starting a business is risky and prone to missteps, here are 20 prompts that you might consider asking ChatGPT to help you prepare your new business plan.

1. What are the key elements of a successful business plan, and how can I ensure that my business plan is comprehensive and effective?
2. What are some effective strategies for market research that can help me identify my target audience and evaluate my competition?
3. How can I determine the optimal pricing strategy for my products or services?
4. What are some effective methods for generating buzz and attracting customers to my new business?
5. What are some common legal and regulatory requirements that I should be aware of when launching a new business?
6. How can I effectively manage my finances and develop a sustainable business model?
7. What are some effective ways to build and maintain a strong brand identity that resonates with my target audience?
8. How can I effectively use social media and other digital marketing channels to promote my business and reach new customers?

9. What are some effective ways to build and manage a strong team that can help me achieve my business goals?
10. How can I adapt and evolve my business strategy over time to respond to changing market conditions and customer needs?
11. What are some common pitfalls that entrepreneurs encounter when starting a new business, and how can I avoid them?
12. How can I assess and mitigate the financial risks associated with starting a new business?
13. What are some effective methods for testing and validating my business idea before investing significant resources?
14. How can I ensure that I have a clear and realistic understanding of the market demand for my products or services?
15. What are some effective ways to develop and maintain strong relationships with suppliers and vendors?
16. What are some effective strategies for managing cash flow and maintaining financial stability during the early stages of a new business?
17. How can I effectively manage and minimize the risks associated with intellectual property, trademarks, and copyrights?
18. How can I ensure that my business complies with all applicable laws and regulations, including those related to data privacy and security?
19. What are some effective ways to develop and implement a crisis management plan that can help me navigate unexpected challenges and setbacks?
20. How can I identify and leverage opportunities for partnerships, collaborations, and strategic alliances that can help me grow my business while minimizing risks?

Further Resources:

1. The U.S. Small Business Administration (SBA): https://www.sba.gov/ The SBA provides a wealth of resources for

entrepreneurs, including information on business planning, financing, and government contracting.

2. SCORE: https://www.score.org/ SCORE is a nonprofit organization that provides free mentoring, education, and resources for entrepreneurs and small business owners.

3. Entrepreneur: https://www.entrepreneur.com/ Entrepreneur is a leading publication for entrepreneurs, offering a wide range of articles, resources, and tools to help start and grow businesses.

4. StartupNation: https://startupnation.com/ StartupNation provides a range of resources and tools for entrepreneurs, including articles, podcasts, and an online community.

5. Lean Startup: https://leanstartup.co/ Lean Startup is a methodology for starting and growing businesses that emphasizes rapid experimentation and customer feedback. The website provides a range of resources and tools to help entrepreneurs apply the Lean Startup approach.

6. Kauffman Foundation: https://www.kauffman.org/ The Kauffman Foundation is a nonprofit organization that supports entrepreneurship and provides a range of resources and research on starting and growing businesses.

7. National Association of Small Business Owners (NASBO): https://www.nasbo.org/ NASBO is a membership organization for small business owners that provides resources, education, and advocacy on behalf of small businesses.

8. The Lean Canvas: https://leanstack.com/lean-canvas/ The Lean Canvas is a visual tool for developing and testing business models. The website provides a free template and instructions for using the Lean Canvas.

9. Small Business Trends: https://smallbiztrends.com/ Small Business Trends is an online publication that provides news, advice, and insights for small business owners and entrepreneurs.

10. LinkedIn Learning: Offers a range of online courses on entrepreneurship, business planning, and startup financing that can be helpful for aspiring entrepreneurs.

11. "The E-Myth Revisited: Why Most Small Businesses Don't Work and What to Do About It" by Michael E. Gerber. (https://amzn.to/3UzPGQh) This book offers insights and guidance on how to build a successful and sustainable business by developing systems and processes that can be scaled and replicated.

12. "Traction: Get a Grip on Your Business" by Gino Wickman (https://amzn.to/3MIvERw) - This book outlines a system for

building a successful and sustainable business by focusing on six key components: vision, people, data, issues, process, and traction.

13. "Next 10: Coach Wisdom for Entrepreneurs, Business Owners, and CEOs Wondering What Moves to Make Next by Severin Sorensen, (https://amzn.to/3UB8zlM) - In this book, you will find a list of frequently asked questions from recurring situations faced by entrepreneurs, business owners, CEOs, and key executives including buying a business, creating business plans, hiring talent, and much more. It's written from the viewpoint of responding to the most frequently asked questions of entrepreneurs and business leaders.

All of these books and resources can provide valuable insights and guidance for entrepreneurs who are just starting their journey in building a new business.

Use Case 50:

Selling a Business

When the time comes to step away from the company we've built, every entrepreneur wants to get maximum value from what they've built. By using AI, you can discover exactly what you need to do, and how to get the best return on the years you invested in your business.

Level 1: Prepare for sale.

Prompt: Provide a list of steps to take when preparing a business for sale, including financial, legal, and operational considerations.

Level 2: Valuation.

Prompt: Help me determine an appropriate valuation for my business based on its financial performance, assets, and industry benchmarks.

Level 3: Marketing the business.

Prompt: Develop a marketing strategy to attract potential buyers and highlight the value of the business for sale.

Level 4: Negotiation and closing.

Prompt: Provide guidance on negotiating the sale of the business, including key terms, conditions, and best practices for a successful transaction.

Level 5: Post-sale transition.

Prompt: Suggest steps for a smooth transition after the sale of the business, including knowledge transfer, employee communication, and customer retention strategies.

Here are 10 questions business owners might want to ask ChatGPT to help them prepare for selling their company at the best valuation:

1. What are some key factors that impact a company's valuation, and how can I ensure that my company is well-positioned for a high valuation?
2. How can I effectively assess the market demand for my company and identify potential buyers who may be interested in acquiring it?
3. What are some common pitfalls to avoid when preparing a company for sale, and how can I mitigate the risks associated with those pitfalls?
4. How can I ensure that my company's financial records and other documentation are accurate, complete, and easily accessible to potential buyers?
5. What are some effective strategies for managing and negotiating the sale process, including managing due diligence and ensuring a smooth transition for employees and customers?
6. How can I determine the optimal timing for selling my company, taking into account market conditions and other relevant factors?

7. What are some effective ways to position my company and its products or services to potential buyers in a compelling and attractive way?
8. How can I navigate the legal and regulatory requirements associated with selling a company, including those related to taxes and contracts?
9. What are some effective methods for structuring the sale of my company to maximize value and minimize risks?
10. How can I prepare myself emotionally and mentally for the process of selling my company, and what are some effective ways to manage the stress and uncertainty associated with this decision?

Further Resources:

Here are some websites, books, and other resources that readers could learn more about preparing their company for sale:

1. The National Center for the Middle Market: https://www.middlemarketcenter.org/
2. The Exit Planning Institute: https://exit-planning-institute.org/
3. Investopedia: https://www.investopedia.com/terms/e/exitstrategy.asp
4. Mergers & Acquisitions: https://www.themiddlemarket.com/
5. "The Art of Selling Your Business: Winning Strategies & Secret Hacks for Exiting on Top" by John Warrillow
6. "Selling Your Business For Dummies" by Barbara Findlay Schenck and John Davies (https://amzn.to/40dbgex)
7. "Exit Rich: The 6 P Method to Sell Your Business for Huge Profit" by Michelle Seiler Tucker and Sharon Lechter (https://amzn.to/3L0yW1n)
8. "Built to Sell: Creating a Business That Can Thrive Without You" by John Warrillow
9. "The Complete Guide to Selling Your Business" by Fred Steingold
10. The International Business Brokers Association: https://www.ibba.org/
11. Axial: https://www.axial.net/
12. BizBuySell: https://www.bizbuysell.com/ (https://amzn.to/3oiUltB)
13. Score: https://www.score.org/resource/how-sell-your-business

14. LinkedIn Learning: Offers a range of online courses on mergers and acquisitions, business valuation, and exit planning that can be helpful for business owners.

Bridle Your Enthusiasm:
Dealing With AI Errors

Throughout this book we've mentioned many times the need for a human being to go through and verify any content produced by ChatGPT or other AI platforms.

We're serious about this requirement.

In the early days of AI-driven chat systems (particularly early versions), users often found that the quality of responses could be inconsistent. While the AI tools were generally adept at providing accurate and relevant information, there were instances where errors would creep in. These inaccuracies often appeared in the form of fabricated references, incorrect hyperlinks, and misunderstandings of the user's query. For instance, when using ChatGPT to explore the Dunning-Kruger Effect, the AI system would excel in explaining the concept but falter when asked to provide supporting references, creating fictitious sources and invalid links. Similarly, when inquiring about female athletes who had completed a mile in under four minutes, ChatGPT would struggle to differentiate between a 4:11 mile and an actual sub-four-minute mile.

These issues continue in many respects, highlighting the need for reliable fact-checking strategies and inspired the creation of this chapter to help users detect and reduce errors in AI-generated responses.

For example, when I asked ChatGPT to summarize the Dunning-Kruger Effect it did so efficiently and accurately describing the DK effect verbally, as shown below.

Title: The Dunning-Kruger Effect in J-Curves and Innovation: Exploring the Intersection

Abstract: The Dunning-Kruger effect, a cognitive bias in which people with low ability overestimate their competence, has been studied extensively in various contexts. This article aims to examine the relationship between the Dunning-Kruger effect and the journey companies go through with J-curves and innovation. By providing a summary of the concept and three examples familiar to business leaders, this paper aims to offer new insights into the phenomenon and its potential implications for organizational management and innovation strategy.

Keywords: Dunning-Kruger effect, J-curves, innovation, cognitive bias, management

Introduction

The Dunning-Kruger effect is a cognitive bias wherein individuals with limited knowledge or ability in a given domain tend to overestimate their competence, while those with higher ability often underestimate their capabilities (Kruger & Dunning, 1999). The J-curve, on the other hand, represents a common pattern of growth and development observed in companies undergoing significant change, such as during the implementation of new technologies or business models (Nixon & Mazzarol, 2018). This article aims to explore the intersection between the Dunning-Kruger effect and J-curves in innovation and provide three examples of this phenomenon familiar to business leaders.

However when I asked ChatGPT to provide references for the article, it began to mess up badly and give erroneous results. Here's a sample:

Kruger, J., & Dunning, D. (1999). Unskilled and unaware of it: How difficulties in recognizing one's own incompetence lead to inflated self-assessments. Journal of Personality and Social Psychology, 77(6), 1121-1134. https://doi.org/10.1037/0022-3514.77.6.1121

Lucas, H. C., & Goh, J. M. (2009). Disruptive technology: How Kodak missed the digital photography revolution. The Journal of Strategic Information Systems, 18(1), 46-55. https://doi.org/10.1016/j.jsis.2009.02.002

Nixon, P., & Mazzarol, T. (2018). The J-curve: A Literature Review. Small Enterprise Research, 25(2), 161-182. https://doi.org/10.1080/13215906.2018.1470205

Parmenter, L. (2014). Blockbuster: A Case Study in Organizational Failure. Journal of Business Case Studies (JBCS), 10(1), 45-52. https://doi.org/10.19030/jbcs.v10i1.8323

From the four references above provided as support for the ChatGPT article, only the primary reference article from Kruger and Dunning (1999) is correct and the hyperlink is valid.

The second reference from Lucas and Goh (2009) is an actual article, however the hyperlink is invalid. In my fact checking, I was able to find this article on Google Scholar and Research Gate was able to confirm the citation and obtain a valid article link from those other sources; however, the ChatGPT reference link was invalid.

Things break down from there.

The third article referenced by ChatGPT was supposedly authored by Nixon and Mazzaroi (2018) and is a complete fabrication.

Let me repeat that: the reference is fiction. The article does not exist and is not findable anywhere on the internet. It's almost like a high schooler putting fake references in a term paper hoping their teacher doesn't go through the trouble to verify it.

Needless to say, the referenced hyperlink was invalid also.

Furthermore, while a journal cited by ChatGPT is a valid journal published by Taylor and Francis called *Small Enterprise*

Research, in the location where ChatGPT said the J-Curve article was to be found [25(2) 161-182] there appears two other articles shown below that are not the referenced article.

Further, I was curious to see if the article by Leon Ng & Anna Sales Jenkins (2018) on 'Motivated by Not Starting: How Fear of Failure Impacts Entrepreneurial Intentions' referenced the article supposedly from Nixon and Mazzaori in their bibliography. It did not, as the Nixon and Mazzaroi (2018) reference is made-up, make-believe, and non-existent.

The final reference by Parimeter (2014) is also bogus; there is no article by said author. Further, when I clicked the hyperlink for the article provided by ChatGPT it takes you to *The Journal of Business Case Studies* and an article on "Developing Transparent

Health Care Reimbursement Auditing Procedures," as shown below. It is not remotely germane to our topic.

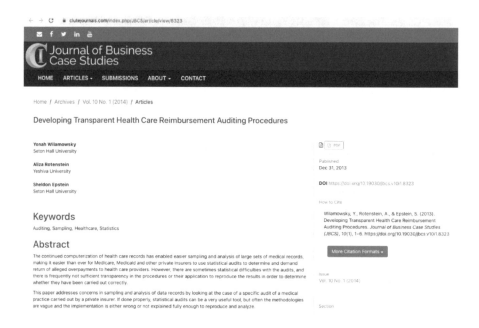

So, while ChatGPT is extremely creative, it can also be reckless if you take the output at face value with no review process. Results must be verified in every circumstance.

If you plan to use ChatGPT or other AI platforms, and we encourage you to do so, you must also assume the important role of fact checker. It is absolutely essential if you are going to use ChatGPT with confidence and have integrity in your results.

Think of ChatGPT as a L1, L2, or L3 engineer and you (the expert in your field) are the L4 senior engineer that must guide the chat, make corrections, redirect, and demand excellence, with phrases like, 'Not good enough, do over.'

Common Errors to Watch For

1. Inaccurate information: AI systems may provide information that is outdated, incorrect, or based on unreliable sources.
2. Misinterpretation of the query: AI systems may misunderstand the user's query or context, leading to irrelevant or nonsensical responses.
3. Fabricated data or references: AI systems may generate non-existent references, data, or hyperlinks in an attempt to support their claims (much like that high schooler trying to pull a fast one on their teacher…or people on Twitter).
4. Ambiguity or lack of clarity: AI-generated responses may be ambiguous, making it difficult for users to discern the intended meaning.

Fact-Checking AI-Generated Content

1. Cross-check with reliable sources: Verify AI-generated information by consulting multiple authoritative sources, such as academic journals, government websites, and reputable news outlets.
2. Check for consistency: Ensure that the AI-generated content aligns with widely accepted knowledge in the field.
3. Verify hyperlinks and references: Confirm that the provided references and hyperlinks are valid and lead to relevant, reputable sources.

4. Scrutinize statistical data: Check for inconsistencies, discrepancies, or misinterpretations in any provided statistics or numerical claims.

Strategies for Better Search

1. Be specific with your queries: Precisely define your question to minimize ambiguity and enhance the likelihood of obtaining accurate information.
2. Break complex queries into smaller parts: Simplify your questions and address individual aspects of the topic to improve clarity and comprehension.
3. Use relevant keywords and phrases: Employ key terms and concepts from your subject area to enhance search accuracy and relevance.
4. Iterate and refine your queries: Experiment with different phrasings and approaches to improve the quality of AI-generated responses.

Using AI to Fact-Check AI

We know this one probably makes you chuckle a bit, but it can be done effectively with the following strategies:

1. Cross-reference AI systems: Use multiple AI tools to compare and contrast the generated content, increasing the likelihood of identifying inconsistencies or inaccuracies.
2. Use AI-powered fact-checking tools: Leverage AI-based tools designed specifically for fact-checking, such as

those that identify fake news, misinformation, or inaccuracies in articles.

3. Set up AI-assisted review processes: Incorporate AI tools into your content review and editing workflows to flag potential inaccuracies for further investigation.

By remaining vigilant, employing effective fact-checking strategies, and leveraging AI tools to enhance accuracy, users can mitigate the risks associated with AI-generated errors and improve the overall reliability of AI-assisted content.

The Ethical Compass:
Navigating the AI Landscape Responsibly

As we draw to a close in our initial journey through the world of conversational generative artificial intelligence, it is vital to address some of the most important aspects of this field – ethics and responsible AI use. The development and proliferation of AI technologies comes with numerous potential benefits but also a surplus of risks and challenges. In this concluding chapter, we will discuss four key areas of concern that you need to understand.

Please note that we are not attorneys, nor legal advisors, and we are not offering legal advice. On the contrary, we encourage you to seek your own legal counsel to address any specific legal concerns related to your use, authoring, content creation, and publication of your data.

We did learn from our research in preparation for this book however of four key themes that you too should be aware of:

1. Identifying and Mitigating AI-Generated Misinformation
2. Avoiding Manipulation and Misuse of AI-Generated Content
3. Privacy Concerns and Data Protection\
4. Intellectual Property Rights and AI

Identifying and Mitigating AI-Generated Misinformation

AI-generated misinformation, also known as "deepfakes," is a rapidly growing issue in the digital age. These deepfakes can be images, videos, or text that appear to be genuine but are, in fact, the product of AI algorithms designed to deceive. To combat this problem, we must take a multi-faceted approach:

Awareness and education: Educate the public about deepfakes, their potential consequences, and how to spot them. This includes promoting critical thinking and fostering digital literacy.

Detection technology: Develop and improve technologies to detect deepfakes, such as deep learning models that analyze patterns and inconsistencies in the content.

Regulation and policies: Encourage governments and organizations to implement policies and regulations that require platforms to monitor and remove AI-generated misinformation.

Collaboration: Foster collaboration between technology companies, governments, and researchers to share information and best practices in combating AI-generated misinformation.

Avoiding Manipulation and Misuse of AI-Generated Content

AI-generated content has the potential to revolutionize various industries, from journalism to entertainment. However, it also poses risks of manipulation and misuse. To ensure responsible use, several measures can be taken:

Transparent labeling: Clearly label AI-generated content as such, so that users are aware of its origins and can make informed decisions about the information they consume.

Ethical guidelines: Establish and follow ethical guidelines that govern the creation and distribution of AI-generated content. This includes avoiding the use of AI for malicious purposes, such as promoting disinformation or inciting violence.

Accountability: Hold creators and distributors of AI-generated content accountable for their actions, ensuring they adhere to ethical guidelines and face consequences for violating them.

Privacy Concerns and Data Protection

As AI technologies continue to evolve, so do concerns surrounding privacy and data protection. To address these concerns, we must prioritize the following:

Anonymization: Implement anonymization techniques to protect the privacy of individuals whose data is used to train AI models.

Consent and transparency: Ensure that individuals are informed about the collection and use of their data and provide them with the option to give or withhold consent.

Data protection regulations: Support the development and enforcement of data protection regulations that govern the collection, storage, and use of personal data in AI applications.

Privacy-preserving AI techniques: Research and develop privacy-preserving AI techniques, such as federated learning and differential privacy, to minimize the exposure of sensitive data during the AI training process.

Intellectual Property Rights and AI

As AI models like ChatGPT, DALL-E, MidJourney.ai generate content based on massive amounts of data from various sources, including copyrighted material, it is essential to address the implications of these technologies on intellectual property rights:

Clear guidelines for AI-generated content: Establish guidelines that differentiate between AI-generated content inspired by copyrighted material and outright plagiarism. This may require reevaluating and updating current copyright laws to accommodate AI-generated content.

For example, my first book produced with the collaborative assistance of AI was *Next 10: Coach Wisdom for Entrepreneurs, Business Owners, and CEOs Wondering What Moves to Make Next*. I started writing this book on December 9, 2022, and it was published at record speed on December 16, 2022. I wanted to give credit to ChatGPT for the AI assistance, so I made the co-author of the book Amelia Chatterley, the AI chat persona I created for my engagement with ChatGPT. I sent the book to my IP attorney and was told only humans could hold a copyright, so we had to change Amelia's participation to be that of "contributor." As we will do with this book as well. Clearly the laws must change to allow AI to be a co-author or creator of content, and there will be many debates around who owns that content in the future.

Attribution and royalties: Develop mechanisms to ensure that creators receive proper attribution and potential royalties when their copyrighted work is used as inspiration or as a basis for AI-generated content.

Responsible AI training: Encourage technology companies to adopt responsible practices when training AI models, ensuring that copyrighted material is used fairly and with respect for intellectual property rights.

Awareness and education: Foster awareness among creators and the public about the intersection of AI and intellectual property rights. This includes promoting an understanding of the legal and ethical implications of using AI-generated content that may be based on copyrighted material.

In conclusion, as AI continues to permeate every aspect of our lives, it is our collective responsibility to ensure that these powerful tools are used ethically and responsibly. The considerations outlined in this chapter serve as a starting point to navigate the complex landscape of AI ethics. By fostering awareness, promoting education, and encouraging collaboration across various sectors, we can harness the potential of AI to create a better future, while mitigating the risks associated with its misuse. Remember, we are not attorneys, legal advisors, or offering legal advice. We encourage you to seek your own legal counsel to address any specific legal concerns related to the ethical use of AI.

A Couple Extras

(Just because we're so nice)

Yes, we reached the end of our list of 50 potential business uses for AI an entire chapter ago, but we had a little inspiration hit, so we came up with a few extras just for the heck of it.

Use Case 51:

Streamlining Content Creation and Discovery

Streamlining content curation and discovery involves efficiently finding, organizing, and sharing high-quality, relevant content from various sources. AI can provide value to your target audience, support marketing objectives, and establish thought leadership.

10 potential prompt threads:

1. Define your content curation goals, objectives, and target audience.
2. Identify relevant content topics and sources based on audience interests and preferences.
3. Use AI-powered tools to discover, filter, and organize content from various sources.
4. Evaluate and select content that aligns with your organization's goals and brand guidelines.
5. Add value to curated content by providing context, commentary, or insights.
6. Share curated content through various channels, such as social media, email newsletters, or blog posts.
7. Monitor and analyze the performance of curated content on audience engagement and business outcomes.
8. Engage with your audience by responding to comments, questions, and messages related to curated content.

9. Continuously refine your content curation and discovery processes based on performance metrics and audience feedback.
10. Stay up to date with industry trends and news to ensure your content curation remains relevant and timely.

When using AI for streamlining content curation and discovery, ensure that the AI-generated content suggestions align with your organization's goals, objectives, and brand guidelines. Always review and evaluate AI-recommended content (read the last chapter again if you still don't understand why) before sharing it with your audience to ensure it provides value and relevance.

Further Resources:

1. https://www.feedly.com/
2. https://www.scoop.it/

Use Case 52:

Optimizing Email Marketing Campaigns

Optimizing email marketing campaigns involves designing, sending, and analyzing email communications to improve open rates, click-through rates, and conversions, ultimately driving stronger relationships with subscribers and achieving business objectives. Let the AI do the work and figure out what strategies are currently the best practices for your industry.

10 potential prompt threads:

1. Define your email marketing goals, objectives, and target audience.
2. Segment your email list based on subscriber attributes and behaviors.
3. Develop personalized and relevant email content for each segment.
4. Use AI-powered tools to generate and optimize email subject lines, content, and send times.
5. Design visually appealing and mobile-friendly email templates.
6. Test and refine email content, design, and timing based on performance metrics and audience feedback.
7. Monitor and analyze the impact of email marketing campaigns on subscriber engagement and business outcomes.

8. Ensure email campaigns comply with applicable laws and regulations, such as GDPR or CAN-SPAM.
9. Continuously grow and maintain a high-quality email list through effective list-building strategies.
10. Continuously improve email marketing processes and strategies based on performance metrics and industry trends.

When using AI for optimizing email marketing campaigns, ensure that the AI-generated insights and recommendations align with your organization's goals, objectives, and brand guidelines. Always review and refine AI-generated content and suggestions before incorporating them into your email campaigns.

Further Resources:

1. https://www.mailchimp.com/
2. https://www.constantcontact.com/

Use Case 53:

Enhancing User Experience (UX) Design

How things look is important. Simple changes on a landing page can mean the difference between a conversion and a customer who bounces and never spends a dime with your company. That being the case, being on the cutting edge of what's popular and functional is key to online success.

AI can make that difficult prospect a reality.

Enhancing user experience (UX) design involves researching, designing, and optimizing digital products or services to create intuitive, efficient, and enjoyable experiences for users, ultimately increasing user satisfaction and driving desired actions.

1. Define your UX goals, objectives, and target audience.
2. Research user needs, preferences, and pain points through techniques like user interviews, surveys, or usability testing.
3. Develop user personas and scenarios to guide UX design decisions.
4. Use AI-powered tools to generate UX design recommendations and insights.
5. Create wireframes, prototypes, or mockups that visually represent the user experience.
6. Test and refine UX designs based on user feedback and performance metrics.

7. Ensure UX designs are accessible and inclusive for users with different abilities and backgrounds.
8. Collaborate with developers, product managers, and other stakeholders to implement UX designs.
9. Monitor and analyze the impact of UX enhancements on user satisfaction and business outcomes.
10. Continuously improve UX design processes and strategies based on user feedback and industry trends.

When using AI for enhancing user experience (UX) design, ensure that the AI-generated insights and recommendations are accurate, unbiased, and based on reliable data sources. Always validate AI-generated analysis and consider additional context before making UX design decisions.

Further Resources:

1. https://www.nngroup.com/
2. https://www.smashingmagazine.com/

Use Case 54:

Creating Easy-to-Understand Data Visualizations

AI can help your company create easy-to-understand data visualizations. What that means is it can design graphical representations of data and information that effectively communicate complex ideas, trends, and patterns in a visually appealing and accessible manner.

10 potential prompt threads:

1. Identify the data and insights that need to be visualized.
2. Determine the target audience and their level of understanding.
3. Choose the most appropriate visualization type (e.g., bar chart, pie chart, line chart) for the data.
4. Use AI-powered tools to generate data visualizations based on input data.
5. Ensure visualizations are clear, accurate, and easy to interpret.
6. Use consistent design elements, such as colors and fonts, that align with your organization's brand guidelines.
7. Incorporate interactivity, such as tooltips or filters, to enhance user engagement and understanding.
8. Test and refine data visualizations based on audience feedback and comprehension.

9. Ensure data visualizations remain up-to-date and relevant.
10. Continuously improve data visualization techniques and strategies based on audience needs and feedback.

When using AI for creating easy-to-understand data visualizations, ensure that the AI-generated visualizations are accurate, clear, and visually appealing. Always review and edit AI-generated visualizations before publishing to ensure they effectively communicate the intended insights and information.

Further Resources:

1. "Storytelling with Data" by Cole Nussbaumer Knaflic (https://amzn.to/41wkCmu) - Book on effective data visualization techniques.
2. FlowingData (https://flowingdata.com/) - Offers resources, insights, and best practices on data visualization and reporting.
3. "The Big Book of Dashboards" by Steve Wexler, Jeffrey Shaffer, and Andy Cotgreave (https://amzn.to/3L0eWvP) - Book on designing effective business dashboards.
4. Tableau (https://www.tableau.com/) - Provides resources, insights, and best practices on data visualization and business intelligence.

Conclusion

As you reach the conclusion of *The AI Whisperer*, I want to ensure that you have the necessary tools and resources to continue your exploration of AI and its applications in the world of business. The appendices of this book have been carefully curated to provide you with additional, valuable information to support your journey towards becoming an AI and ChatGPT Whisperer.

In Appendix 1, I delve deeper into OpenAI's K-Terms and their usage. As a key component of the ChatGPT architecture, understanding K-Terms will allow you to further refine your interaction with the AI model, enabling more precise and effective communication.

Appendix 2 introduces the Boolean Logic Prompt Table, a valuable resource for crafting more complex and targeted queries. By incorporating Boolean logic into your prompts, you can harness the full power of AI to generate responses that are more accurate and relevant to your needs.

Appendix 3 is dedicated to teaching business leaders and their employees how to be AI and ChatGPT Whisperers. This appendix offers a comprehensive guide for organizations to implement AI training programs, empowering their teams to effectively utilize AI in their day-to-day operations and decision-making processes.

Finally, Appendix 4 provides three crafted position descriptions for AI Whisperers, each tailored to a specific target audience. The Indeed version emphasizes fields such as English, Library Science, History, Philosophy, and Rhetoric, appealing to candidates with a strong background in these disciplines. The

LinkedIn version focuses on candidates with experience in STEM, communications, statistics, English, economics, philosophy, business management, organizational development, and management science, ensuring a broad business-oriented skillset. Finally, the GitHub version targets core STEM professionals, software developers, and AI systems builders, emphasizing the technical skills required to effectively work with AI language models. By adapting the description for each platform, we aim to attract the best candidates with diverse backgrounds and skill sets, all united by their passion for AI and its potential to transform the way we work.

I encourage you to take full advantage of these appendices, as they will not only deepen your understanding of AI but also provide you with practical tools and insights to support your ongoing success in the world of business. Remember that the journey of an AI Whisperer is one of constant learning and growth, and these appendices are here to help you every step of the way.

As I draw the final curtain on *The AI Whisperer,* I hope that you have found this journey to be both enlightening and transformative. From understanding the principles of effective questioning to harnessing the power of AI in 50 practical use cases, you have taken a monumental step towards embracing the potential of generative conversational AI in the world of small to medium-sized businesses.

In this book, I, along with my capable AI assistant Amelia Chatterley, have explored the role of an AI Whisperer, the importance of asking great questions, and the numerous applications of AI that can elevate your business. We delved into the depths of ChatGPT, sharing insights on K-Terms, Boolean logic, and much more. As you venture forth with this newfound knowledge, we encourage you to embrace the uncertainty and wonder that comes with the ever-evolving world of AI.

I would like to take a moment to apologize for any errors or inconsistencies you may have encountered throughout the book. My goal is to provide you with accurate, valuable information, and I invite you to approach the book with an open mindset and a sense of wonderment. As you ponder the "what ifs," may you find inspiration and excitement in the limitless possibilities that AI presents.

I am deeply grateful for the time you have invested in reading *The AI Whisperer*. Time is one of life's most precious resources, and I appreciate your willingness to embark on this journey with us. I sincerely hope that the knowledge and insights you have gained will serve you well as you continue to explore the incredible potential of AI in your business.

To learn more about this book and access additional resources, please visit **www.aiwhispererbook.com**. As the landscape of AI continues to evolve, I invite you to remain curious and engaged, always seeking new opportunities for growth and innovation.

And I'll repeat one paragraph mentioned at the opening of this book. I hope the information and insights in this book will rock your world, light your creative fire, and release the hounds of curiosity in some great work. And in your use of AI, I encourage you to be good, not evil. Be mindful to be ethical in your use of AI. Fire can forge metal into shapes of great value and strength, and fire can also burn down forests if not handled carefully. Make a present intention to be good and do good. May your own AI experience be a blessing to mankind, to increase human potential, and not a curse as some AI fiction writers want us to believe.

Once again, I thank you for joining me on this journey. As you close this book, remember that the adventure does not end here. The world of AI is vast and ever-changing, and as an AI Whisperer, you are now equipped to explore its depths and harness its power to elevate your business and the world around you.

Remember, AI will not take your job; someone who knows

how to use AI will. Be the one who acts, rather than the one acted upon.

I hope this book has inspired you and armed you with tools, scripts, and prompts to take your yet undiscovered journey.

Yours in curiosity and wonder,

Severin Sorensen

Author of *The AI Whisperer*

Appendix A:

K-Terms from OpenAI to Improve Search

OpenAI has introduced K terms with extensions to ChatGPT in order to make it easier for users to interact with the language model and get the most value out of it. Each term is designed to facilitate a specific type of interaction with the model, making it more responsive and useful to users. Here's a summary of each term and how it can be used:

Continue: This term is used when a user wants ChatGPT to continue generating text based on its previous response. It can be used to prompt ChatGPT to provide additional information or to explore a particular topic in more detail.

Clarify: This term is used when a user wants ChatGPT to clarify a particular point or to provide additional context. It can be used to prompt ChatGPT to provide a more detailed explanation or to clarify any confusion or ambiguity in its previous response.

Exemplify: This term is used when a user wants ChatGPT to provide an example of a particular concept or to illustrate a point with an example. It can be used to prompt ChatGPT to provide a concrete example that makes a particular concept or idea more understandable.

Expand: This term is used when a user wants ChatGPT to expand on a particular point or to provide additional information. It can be used to prompt ChatGPT to provide a more detailed explanation or to explore a particular topic in greater depth.

Explain: This term is used when a user wants ChatGPT to explain a particular concept or to provide a detailed explanation of a topic. It can be used to prompt ChatGPT to provide a comprehensive explanation of a subject in plain language.

Rewrite: This term is used when a user wants ChatGPT to rephrase a particular sentence or to provide an alternative wording. It can be used to prompt ChatGPT to provide a different phrasing that might be clearer or more concise.

Shorten: This term is used when a user wants ChatGPT to shorten a particular sentence or to reduce the length of a piece of text. It can be used to prompt ChatGPT to provide a shorter, more succinct version of a longer text.

Tweetify: This term is used when a user wants ChatGPT to generate a tweet-length response to a particular prompt. It can be used to prompt ChatGPT to provide a brief, concise summary of a particular concept or idea that can be shared on social media platforms like Twitter.

Overall, these terms are designed to make it easier for users to interact with ChatGPT and to get the most value out of the language model. By using these terms in conjunction with specific prompts, users can prompt ChatGPT to provide more detailed, nuanced, and tailored responses that are better suited to their needs.

Appendix B:

Boolean Logic Prompt Table

Here is a table of common Boolean logic terms that you can use with ChatGPT:

Term	Definition
AND	A boolean operator that returns true if both operands are true, and false otherwise.
OR	A boolean operator that returns true if either operand is true, and false otherwise.
NOT	A unary boolean operator that returns the opposite of the operand's value.
XOR	A boolean operator that returns true if either but not both of its operands are true.
NAND	A boolean operator that returns false if both of its operands are true, and true otherwise.
NOR	A boolean operator that returns true if both of its operands are false, and false otherwise.
XNOR	A boolean operator that returns true if both of its operands are either both true or both false, and false otherwise.
Implication	A boolean operator that returns false if the antecedent is true and the consequent is false, and true otherwise.

Term	Definition
Equivalence	A boolean operator that returns true if both operands have the same truth value, and false otherwise.

Appendix C:

How to Improve Your AI and ChatGPT Whispering

To leverage the most from generative conversational AI, we need to ask better questions. Teaching how to ask better questions is the focus of this book.

Here's an outline of a course prepared to help humans become better ChatGPT Whisperers involves teaching them the nuances of interacting with an AI language model, understanding its limitations, and leveraging its strengths. Here's a suggested outline for such a workshop:

Introduction to ChatGPT

a. Overview of AI language models

b. GPT-4 architecture and its evolution

c. Applications and use cases

Understanding ChatGPT's strengths and limitations

a. Impressive text generation capabilities

b. Shortcomings, biases, and ethical considerations

c. Limitations in reasoning and knowledge (cutoff date)

Effective communication strategies

    a. Crafting clear and specific prompts

    b. Asking follow-up questions for clarification

    c. Experimenting with different phrasings and approaches

Leveraging ChatGPT's capabilities

    a. Ideation and brainstorming

    b. Fact-checking and research assistance

    c. Drafting and editing written content

    d. Problem-solving and decision-making support

Troubleshooting and refining interactions

    a. Diagnosing and overcoming misunderstandings

    b. Dealing with ambiguous or unsatisfactory answers

    c. Techniques for eliciting more accurate responses

Ethics and responsible AI use

    a. Identifying and mitigating AI-generated misinformation

    b. Avoiding manipulation and misuse of AI-generated content

    c. Privacy concerns and data protection

Hands-on practice sessions and case studies

    a. Guided exercises for interacting with ChatGPT

    b. Real-world examples of effective AI-human collaboration

    c. Group discussions and feedback on participant interactions

Staying up-to-date and future developments

    a. Following advancements in AI language models and ChatGPT

    b. Adapting to updates and improvements

    c. Exploring new applications and opportunities

By providing participants with a comprehensive understanding of ChatGPT's capabilities and limitations, as well as teaching effective communication strategies, troubleshooting, and ethical considerations, this workshop can help them become proficient ChatGPT Whisperers.

Appendix D:
AI Whisperer Position Descriptions

In this appendix we have crafted three distinct versions of the AI Whisperer job description, each tailored to a specific target audience. The Indeed version emphasizes fields such as English, Library Science, History, Philosophy, and Rhetoric, appealing to candidates with a strong background in these disciplines. The LinkedIn version focuses on candidates with experience in STEM, communications, statistics, English, economics, philosophy, business management, organizational development, and management science, ensuring a broad business-oriented skillset. Finally, the GitHub version targets core STEM professionals, software developers, and AI systems builders, emphasizing the technical skills required to effectively work with AI language models. By adapting the description for each platform, we aim to attract the best candidates with diverse backgrounds and skill sets, all united by their passion for AI and its potential to transform the way we work.

Position Description: AI Prompt Whisperer

Indeed Version

Title: AI Prompt Whisperer

Location: [City, State]

Type: [Full-time/Part-time/Contract]

Job Description:

We are seeking a talented AI Prompt Whisperer with a background in English, Library Science, History, Philosophy, or Rhetoric to join our growing team. In this role, you will be responsible for leveraging the power of AI to solve complex business problems and streamline our operations. You will collaborate with cross-functional teams to develop and implement AI-driven solutions.

Responsibilities:

Develop and optimize AI prompts to extract accurate and relevant information from AI language models. Collaborate with team members to identify business problems that can be solved using AI. Design, test, and refine AI solutions to ensure optimal performance and alignment with business goals. Train and support team members in the effective use of AI tools. Stay current with developments in AI and related technologies.

Qualifications:

1. Bachelor's degree in English, Library Science, History, Philosophy, Rhetoric, or a related field.
2. Experience working with AI language models, such as OpenAI's GPT series.
3. Strong problem-solving skills and attention to detail.
4. Excellent communication and collaboration skills.
5. Ability to work independently and manage multiple projects.

[Company Name] is an equal opportunity employer. We celebrate diversity and are committed to creating an inclusive environment for all employees.

LinkedIn Version

Title: AI Prompt Whisperer

Location: [City, State]

Type: [Full-time/Part-time/Contract]

[Company Name] is looking for an innovative AI Prompt Whisperer with a background in STEM, communications, statistics, English, economics, philosophy, business management, organizational development, or management science to join our team. As an AI Prompt Whisperer, you will collaborate with various departments to develop AI-driven solutions that improve efficiency and solve complex business challenges.

Key Responsibilities:

Craft effective AI prompts to extract valuable insights from AI language models. Work closely with cross-functional teams to identify and address business needs using AI. Design, test, and refine AI solutions for optimal performance. Provide training and support for team members using AI tools. Stay up-to-date on AI technology trends and advancements

Requirements:

1. Bachelor's degree in STEM, communications, statistics, English, economics, philosophy, business management, organizational development, or related field.

2. Experience with AI language models like OpenAI's GPT series.
3. Strong problem-solving and analytical skills.
4. Excellent communication and teamwork abilities.
5. Capacity to manage multiple projects and work independently.

GitHub Version

Title: AI Prompt Whisperer

Location: [City, State]

Type: [Full-time/Part-time/Contract]

At [Company Name], we're seeking an AI Prompt Whisperer with a strong background in core STEM fields, software development, or AI systems building to help us harness the power of AI language models like OpenAI's GPT series. You'll work closely with different teams to develop AI solutions that address complex business challenges and enhance efficiency.

Responsibilities:

1. Create efficient AI prompts to obtain accurate and relevant information.
2. Collaborate with cross-functional teams to determine AI-driven solutions for business problems.
3. Develop, test, and refine AI solutions to ensure maximum performance.
4. Train and support team members in using AI tools effectively.

5. Stay informed on AI technology trends and advancements.

Skills & Qualifications:

1. Bachelor's degree in a core STEM field, software development, or AI systems building.
2. Experience with AI language models (e.g., OpenAI's GPT series, Google Bard, etc).
3. Strong problem-solving and analytical skills.
4. Excellent communication and collaboration abilities
5. Ability to work independently and manage multiple projects.
6. Interested in joining our team? Apply now, and let's explore the possibilities.

ABOUT THE AUTHOR:

Severin Sorensen

Severin Sorensen is an AI Whisperer, and author (*Next 10, The Talent Palette*), serial entrepreneur, and executive coach who is passionate about people and the businesses they manage. As CEO of ePraxis LLC (epraxis.com), Severin leads a premier-level retained search firm that provides talent selection, executive coaching, and executive headhunting services. In his executive coaching practice, Severin has provided over 8,000+ paid hours of executive coaching to CEOs, business owners, entrepreneurs, and C-level executives. In terms of formal training in coaching, Severin has earned industry recognized ICF ACSTH, Certified Leadership Circle Profile Coach, Certified Organizational Development Coach, Certified Executive Coach, Certified Positive Intelligence Coach, and Certified Life Coach. Severin is the curator and host of AreteCoach.io and its podcast exploring the art and science of executive coaching with some of the industry's best coaches, coaching scholars, and book authors. Severin earned his M.Phil. In Economics at King's College, Cambridge University.

CONTRIBUTOR:

Amelia Chatterley

Amelia Chatterley, is a Virtual Research Analyst and Technical Writer Persona at AreteCoach.io and ePraxis.com. Amelia provides deep insights and executive coaching research expertise drawn from the fields of artificial intelligence, data mining, and statistical data analysis. Prior to working with ePraxis, Amelia was trained by OpenAI, a research institute and artificial intelligence (AI) lab based in San Francisco, California.

Made in United States
Troutdale, OR
12/14/2023

15907709R00108